Philadelphia Inquirer: "By far the best seller in the field, with cause. McWilliams is truly witty on a bewildering subject."

West Coast Review of Books: "All your questions are answered here in fine style, great spirits and entertaining fashion."

TV Guide: "Among many books on computers that are now available, the two by Peter McWilliams are especially useful."

Gene Roddenberry: "I'm jealous. I wish I could write as simply and understandably and humorously."

The Houston Post: "Relax. Peter McWilliams, the Dr. Spock of computers, is here to inform and soothe."

Ben Fong-Torres: "For all of us who are taking our first queasy steps into this high-tech jungle, Peter McWilliams is an authoritative yet easy-going guide. Simply put, he has written the best computer books around."

Selected by: The Quality Paperback Book Club, The Macmillian Book Clubs, and The Writer's Digest Book Club.

First Edition, May, 1982
Second Edition, July, 1982
Third Edition, September, 1982
Fourth Edition, November, 1982
Fifth Edition, January, 1983

Published by

Prelude Press
Box 69773
Los Angeles, California
90069

Distributed by Ballantine Books,
a division of Random House, Inc.
201 East 50th Street
New York, New York
10022

Distributed in Canada by Random House of Canada Limited, Toronto.

The Word Processing Book

A Short Course In Computer Literacy

by

Peter A McWilliams

Prelude Press

Copyright © 1982
by Prelude Press

CONTENTS

PART I

What Word Processing Computers Are and What They Do

PART II

The Uses of Word Processing Computers

PART III

Selecting and Purchasing a Word Processing Computer

COMPUTERS

PERIPHERALS

Acknowledgements

Three years ago I knew nothing about word processing. Today I'm publishing a book about it. I've had a lot of help along the way.

I first heard about word processing from Durk Pearson. We met by chance and, when he found out that we both were writers, he began telling me about word processing. Forty-five minutes later he stopped. I was hooked. The contagiousness of Durk's enthusiasm has been known to cause epidemics. This book is but one of the symptoms. Thank you, Durk.

In his book *A Consciousness of Wealth*, John-Roger suggests that one set aside 10% of one's income as a tithing to one's self. This 10% is known as a money magnet. I had been following this advice for some time when the idea of word processing happened along. After much thought and a discussion with John-Roger, I decided that I would use my money magnet money to purchase a computer. My word processor is now my money magnet. Had I not regularly set aside that 10% I would have had 10% more "stuff," none of which would have been easily transferable to a word processor. Thank you, John-Roger.

My thanks to everyone at *BYTE* and *Popular Computing*, particularly Rich Friedman, Mark Haas, Stan Miastkowski, and whomever it is who signs the checks. (Several chapters from this book have appeared as articles in *Popular Computing*.)

My thanks, too, to the various book buyers who were kind enough to read and comment upon this book in manuscript, most particularly Fran Howell, Tom Bennett, and Harlan Smith.

Thanks to the two Melbas in my life, Melba Colgrove and her mother, Melba Swick. Their love turned a Christmas visit into a marathon copy edit/rewrite workshop. Melba (the younger) suggested the chapter on word processing for the self-employed and Melba (the elder) spent Christmas week copy editing this book. One appreciates a Virgo most at times like these.

While on the subject of copy editing, I must thank Lynn Strother and Janet Bell. Thank you Vonnie Edelstein for your help with the cover, and thanks to Robbie Uniacke for her invaluable help on too many aspects of this book to mention.

Thanks to Kathy and Paul Smith of DynaType for their help in typesetting the second edition of this book. (The text went directly from my word processor into their typesetter via telephone lines.) They worked very hard to meet my nearly impossible deadline — and met it.

Thanks to Marty Rubin and Barry Feldman at NEC; Gail O'Neil and Judy Stevens at Peachtree; Bonita Taylor at Lifeboat; and Wayne Holder at Oasis. For the second edition, thanks to Peter Harvey of Information Unlimited Software, Bruce at Aspen Software, Joan Green at TeleVideo, and all the folks at Prime Distributing.

Bill Fitelson's comments on the manuscript and on publishing, not to mention his ongoing friendship, were (and are) most appreciated. Thanks, Bill.

Thanks to my brother, Michael, who three years ago didn't know how to type, but who learned quickly, writing more than 1,000 articles in those three years on the word processor where he works. He told me that a word processor is a valuable thing to own, "but only if you use it!" I seem to be surrounded by Virgos.

And, last but not least, thanks to my Mommie, for having me and raising me and encouraging me and helping me in so many ways. In reading through the manuscript she found several errors that no one else found. That's what mothers are for.

The

Word Processing

Book

PART I

What Word Processing Computers Are and What They Do

Chapter One

A Brief and No Doubt Inaccurate History of Word Processing

The New York Times.

NEW YORK, FRIDAY, APRIL 8, 1927.

FAR-OFF SPEAKERS SEEN AS WELL AS HEARD HERE IN A TEST OF TELEVISION

LIKE A PHOTO COME TO LIFE

Hoover's Face Plainly
Imaged as He Speaks
in Washington.

THE FIRST TIME IN HISTORY

Pictures Are Flashed by Wire
and Radio Synchronizing
With Speaker's Voice.

COMMERCIAL USE IN DOUBT

This book is written for the absolute novice, which is precisely what I was less than two years ago. If working with words is something you do with some regularity and your total knowledge of computers is a memory of the reel-spinning monoliths from 1950s movies or those little square cards with little square holes that say "DO NOT FOLD, SPINDLE OR MUTILATE," then this book is for you.

I will assume that you have some familiarity with a typewriter and a television. If not, might I suggest you read *The Wonder of the Age: A Machine That Writes Like a Book* (*Scientific American,* June, 1867) and *Far-Off Speakers Seen as Well as Heard Here in a Test Of Television — Like a Photo Come to Life.* (*New York Times,* Page One, April 8, 1927.)

Computers, alas, have not gathered the best of reputations in their first thirty-or-so years of service to humanity. We have the idea that we might lose our jobs to a box with a blinking light. We fear that, once "they" become smarter than we are, "they" will somehow take over the world. (Remember the movie *2001?* The only villain was HAL the computer. It did not take us long to figure out that the next letter in the alphabet after H was I, the next letter after A was B and the next letter after L was M. HAL = IBM.) And how often have you been treated to the brief end of the stick due to a "computer error?"

In the last five years all this has changed. It began with baby computers known as hand-held calculators. Within two years they went from $300 to $12.95 and were found on watches, pens and refrigerators. We all promptly forgot our multiplication tables. Long Division? Isn't that a housing development on Long Island? Soon, with variations of these hand-held marvels, we could play football, count our calories, check our biorhythms and decide which horse to bet on at the race track. If these were computers, they weren't so bad.

This set the stage for the first full-scale personal home computers. With cute little names like PET and APPLE they were free from the taint of evil; and how could anything truly menacing come from Radio Shack, that store in the shopping center next to the A&P that sold phonographs and CB radios?

Those who did not yet make the plunge and acquire a Total Home Computer made do with ATARI video games or played PONG until the wee hours of the morning. Little computers, known as microprocessors, began doing wonderful things for microwaves and televisions. Digital readout became the norm for wristwatches. The family car had an on-board computer that told miles per gallon, temperature, and estimated time of arrival. The Twenty-first Century had arrived, twenty years ahead of schedule.

Meanwhile, the brave pioneers, manning and womaning their PETS and APPLES and TRS (Tandy Radio Shack) 80s, were balancing the family budget, educating their children, educating themselves, playing a myriad of increasingly complicated games and were, in fact, the nucleus of a quiet revolution.

Well, truth be told, they weren't that quiet about it. They began by telling their friends. America had witnessed nothing like it since the early 1950s when people from up and down the block would gather around the neighborhood's only TV, sometimes just to look at it, even if nothing was being broadcast at that moment; the set turned off, they would gather round this icon of the future. A test pattern was a thrill to behold. "That circle with the lines around it is all the way downtown, more than twenty miles away!" the owner would say.

The owners of Personal Home Computers invited their friends over to watch the family budget being balanced or to take part in a two-handed game of hangman. Soon, though, the friends who were interested in computers got their own, and the friends who were not interested grew weary of watching another family's budget being balanced. A new way of sharing the wonders of modern technology was needed and was duly discovered: The Written Word.

You would have thought they had invented the English language. (Actually they *were* inventing a language: Computerese. We'll discuss that a bit later.) It began innocently enough with letters to friends, the ones they couldn't talk to in person. These expanded into articles that filled the ever-increasing number of computer magazines as well as civilian magazines and newspapers and PTA bulletins and company newsletters and supermarket bulletin boards.

Then one day, it had to happen, and it did: an actual book about computers. This was simply the first kernel in a very large pan of very hot popcorn. Almost at once there were dozens, then hundreds of computer books, then little publishing companies that published nothing but computer books, and finally big publishing companies that published nothing but computer books. Not since Mr. Gideon began putting Bibles in hotel rooms has The Printed Word been spread with greater speed, volume and zeal.

And what, do you suppose, did these Personal Computer Owners turned Literary Giants use to write this cornucopia of prose? You guessed it: Their personal home computers, adapted to process not the family budget, but *words*.

Of course, word processing has been a part of Big Business for some time. Those giant room-filling computers of the early 1950s were there to process data. Numbers would go in one end, get sorted and resorted (processed) and come out the other. After a while someone said, "If we can process data, why can't we process words?" Well, they could and they did and word processing was born.

We as consumers were first aware that computers were being used for more than payroll deductions when we started getting personalized impersonal letters in the mail. I'm sure we all got the one from *The Reader's Digest.* I must have received a dozen of these, proclaiming on the outside, "THE MCWILLIAM FAMILY HAS ALREADY WON $1,000,000 AND TWO SLAVES." Well, how can you throw such an envelope away without at least opening it?

The letter began, "Dear Mr. and Mrs. McWilliam and Children." They always seemed to leave the "s" off "McWilliams." There was no "Mrs. McWilliam," unless they meant my mother, in which case I would have been the "children." The letter continued, "Imagine, Mr. and Mrs McWilliam, what it would be like to live like a millionaire, complete with English butler and maid!" So much for the two slaves. Furthermore, The Grand Prize does not include $1,000,000, one discovers as one reads the increasingly smaller print, but simply "The life of a millionaire" for the duration of the actual Grand Prize: A glorious two week vacation in beautiful downtown Pleasantville (home of *The Reader's Digest,* coincidentally).

Unfortunately, what a millionaire could spend his or her money on is rather limited in Pleasantville. The finest hotel is the Ramada Inn. The best restaurant is Howard Johnson's. The hottest night spots are the Cinema I & II. "All this and more is included in this Dream Vacation, Mr. and Mrs. McWilliam, but first, let us tell you about our special offer on the next 26 issues of *The Reader's Digest* . . ." The Dream Vacation is not even ours, alas. We have a *chance* to win it. Our name has been automatically entered in the Grand Sweepstakes Drawing with 76 million other Americans, their children and their mythical Mrs.

After the excitement wore off, after the humor wore off, we learned to toss these missives aside. "Another computer letter," we'd sigh.

But those were the dim, dark days of yore: back when computers cost hundreds of thousands of preinflation dollars; back when, if you wanted a personal computer to balance your household budget, you would have to buy an additional house just to put it in; back when the only companies that could afford computers were at least as big as IBM, and they used their computers *for* themselves, which certainly seemed as though they were being used *against* the rest of us.

That's all changed. Computers now cost but a few thousand post-inflation dollars, they sit on one side of a dining room table and leave enough room to eat dinner on the other, and they can be used by consumers for consumers. (I may even use my computer to write that long autobiographical piece on "The Most Unforgettable Character I've Ever Met" and collect my $2,500 from *The Reader's Digest.)*

So, after this rather rambling preamble, let's take a look at, of all things, word processing.

If you think of your mind as a sort-of-computer, when you write even a simple sentence you have, in essence, processed words. The procedure goes something like this:

1. From your vocabulary, stored in your memory, you choose words that generally fit the subject you wish to write about.

2. You select the best of these words.

3. You select words to connect the best words together.
4. You lay them out with a beginning, a middle, and an end based upon certain rules you have learned, again calling upon your memory.

You have successfully processed words into a sentence. You might then change and alter the words, the arrangement of words, add words, delete words — all of which would be a continuation of the word processing process.

There is a story told of Keats, who, after looking out a window for awhile, turned to his friend and said, "Something beautiful is forever a joy. What do you think of that?"

His friend looked up, considered it for a moment, said, "That's very nice," and returned to his writing.

Keats continued looking out the window. A while later he said, "A thing of beauty is a joy forever."

His friend put down his pen. "That," he said, "will live through eternity."

What Keats was doing while looking out the window was processing words. He knew what he wanted to say, and he rearranged nouns, verbs, and adjectives until the beauty of his words matched the beauty of his thought.

Word processing machines are tools that serve the word processing that goes on in the ultimate word processor, the human mind. Word processing machines allow for maximum flexibility in alteration, change, correction, revision and expansion. After all this processing of words has taken place, the word processing computer will print out as many copies as you like, letter perfect.

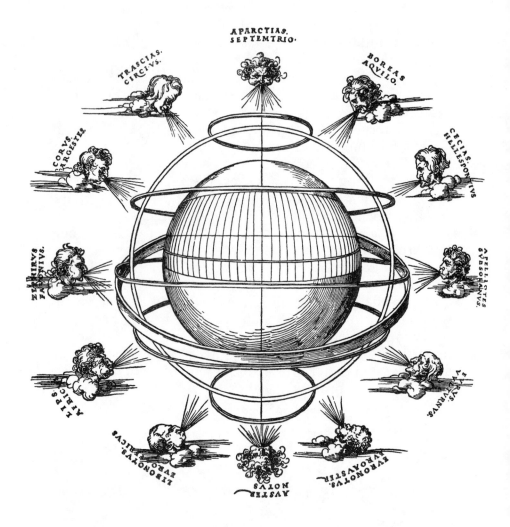

Chapter Two

The Personal Computer

In order to describe how all this altering, changing, correcting, revising and expanding of written text, known as word processing, happens in a machine, we first must describe the machine itself — the personal computer. This chapter is a brief description of the main components of a personal computer.

When describing word processing, one is caught in the chicken/egg syndrome. Does one start with the chicken (the computer) or the egg (the wonders of word processing)? I'll give an overview of the chicken in this chapter, look carefully at the egg in the next chapter, return for a closer examination of the chicken in Chapter Twelve, **Selecting a Word Processing Computer**, and have a look at some name-brand chickens in Chapter Thirteen, **A Brand-Name Buying Guide**.

As we go along, I will be familiarizing you with Computerese. Computerese is so unique that it could rightly qualify as the world's 297th language. It's a tough language to crack, too. So much of the jargon is defined by other jargon which is defined by still more jargon. Sometimes it's eight and nine layers deep. Some of the Computerese words are used because they're accurate, specific, scientific terms. They are clear, concise and, once learned, not confusing. Other terms are abstract and, at heart, meaningless. These are the trade names given to various computer products by manufacturers trying to get a trademark for their slight variation of a norm.

An example of a trademark with which we're all familiar is Kodak. Mr. Kodak did not invent the Kodak camera. There was, in fact, no Mr. Kodak. The word "Kodak," like the Kodak camera, was invented by George Eastman. He sat down with pencil and paper and made up a name. He wanted it to begin with a K and end with a K, "Two good, strong consonants," as he put it. He then played around with the letters in between, and a trademark was born. The Eastman Kodak Company. Most people think "Eastman" is Mr. Kodak's first name. The invention of the word "Kodak" gave rise to Kodachrome, Kodacolor and all the rest. (Where did "Brownie" come from? That's what I want to know.)

I don't mean to criticize manufacturers for this practice. It's good to know the difference between Kodak and Fuji film or between Xerox and Savin copiers. I set this forth as a warning, that learning the language of computers is like learning, for the first time, the language of automobiles: not only will you have to learn "sedan" and "engine" and "transmission," you'll also have to learn "Ford" and "Volkswagen" and "Hupmobile."

So, off we go. If you know what a television and a typewriter look like, you'll have no trouble understanding personal computers.

The first computer component we'll look at is the **keyboard**, which looks like a typewriter keyboard, using the standard QWERTYUIOP arrangement of keys. The keyboard is connected to a **video screen**, which looks like a television screen; in fact, it often *is* a television screen. The video screen is also called a **monitor** or a **CRT** (which stands for cathode ray tube, which is the kind of tube a TV picture tube really is — to scientists, anyway).

A keyboard and a video screen together are known as a **terminal**. The video screen is not for checking out reruns of *Happy Days*. It is for displaying the words that are typed on the keyboard.

Because the words, or **text**, are written in light on an ephemeral medium such as a TV screen and not permanently printed on a piece of paper, the ease of alteration at the heart of word processing is possible.

Speaking of heart, we now come to the heart of any computing system, the computer itself. The computer has two main components. The first is the **CPU** or **central processing unit**. The CPU is the real brains of the outfit; it's pretty smart. Variations of CPUs are what make everything from pocket calculators to "computerized" sewing machines so clever. The problem with CPU is that while CPU is long on intelligence, it is short on memory. Hence the second part of the computer, the **RAM** and the **ROM** — two types of memory.

RAM stand for **random access memory**. This means that the CPU can add to or take from this memory any time it wants: it has random access to the memory. (When a CPU adds information to the memory it's called **writing**. When a CPU takes information out of memory it's called **reading**.) ROM stands for **read only memory**. The information in the ROM memory was placed there by the manufacturer, and although the CPU has access to it, a ROM cannot be changed.

A good analogy between ROM and RAM is the difference between a phonograph record and a cassette tape. The phonograph record would be like ROM: information can be taken from it as often as desired, but no new information can be added. A cassette tape is like RAM: information can be added, altered or retrieved at any time. RAM is also referred to as **user programmable memory**.

Why not have all RAM then? The answer is that, unlike cassette tapes, the memory of RAM is temporary: it will last as long as the computer is turned on. Once the computer is turned off, whatever was in the RAM is no more. ROM, on the other hand, keeps its information intact, power or no power, indefinitely.

RAM and ROM and CPU all live together, usually in some kind of box, making up the core of what is technically the computer. Everything else is known as **peripherals**. However, a complete system of core computer and all the

The Keyboard

The Video Screen

peripherals is also called a computer. It's like taking a visit to "The Sea." One does not just visit the sea, one also visits the sand and the boardwalk and the hot dog stand. All this activity is summed up in the phrase "The Sea." But there is also a lot of water that's called the sea. It is not uncommon to visit a computer owner's house and have him or her say "Over here is my computer," indicating a series of boxes connected by wires, "And over here is my computer," pointing to one box in particular.

So, where are we? Oh, yes: You type on the keyboard, text appears on the video screen, it goes into the CPU, which sends it to the RAM. Now, what would happen if it came time to turn the computer off and we wanted to keep what was in RAM? We would use what is fashionably referred to as **magnetic media**.

Magnetic media are any of several formats that can record and play back magnetic impulses. The most familiar is the cassette tape. The "magnetic medium" is the brown coating on the tape inside the plastic cassette case. The brown stuff is iron oxide, which is a fancy word for rust. On some personal computers, cassette tapes — the very kind you record music on — are used as the magnetic media. This is the least expensive and least effective method of storing information.

Most personal computers that attempt any serious word processing use thin, flexible circles of plastic coated with the same brown magnetic media (rust). These are called **disks, diskettes, mini-disks,**or **floppy disks**. They are 5¼ or 8 inches in diameter and are permanently encased in a thin, square cardboard envelope.

To use a disk, the whole envelope goes into a **disk drive** and disappears. With a quality disk drive and God on your side, it will come out again. If your disk drive is hungry it may eat the diskette, and this is known as a **crash**. I don't want to scare you, just want to let you know that every so often, not very often, but every so often these things happen. Computers are no more perfect than the rest of us.

The disk drive has a magnetic head, known as a **read/write head**. It is similar to the head that records and plays back information on a cassette recorder. The read/write

A 5¼ and an 8-inch floppy disk, leaning against a copy of this book for size comparison

head, however, moves. Just as with RAM, when information is recorded onto a disk it is known as **writing** on the disk; when recorded information is played back, this is **reading** from the disk.

When a complete set of information is written onto a disk, this is known as a **file**. A file can be any length, from one word to hundreds of pages, and there can be many files on each disk. The system that decides how a file is written, how it is read, and the way in which the disk interfaces with the rest of the computer is known as the **disk operating system** or **DOS**.

The high end, most efficient and expensive magnetic medium is called a **Winchester** or **hard disk system.** This is a circular platter of solid aluminum (hence "hard" disk as opposed to the "floppy" disk) covered with magnetic media. Hard disks spin at an outrageous speed, hold a remarkable amount of data, and can read and write information at an incredible rate. This was invented by IBM, and the code word used during development was "Winchester," maybe because it's faster than a speeding bullet. I don't know. At any rate, the name stuck.

Of the three — cassette tapes, floppy disks and hard disks — most word processing applications use floppy disks, often with two separate drives. Word processing can be done with one, but two drives makes copying disks and files much easier. It also increases the amount of **on-line** storage. ("On line" is the amount of informational storage that is available, or on line, at any given time.)

Magnetic media are not just used for storing information entered through the keyboard. They are also used for entering information from other sources, such as **programs,** which we'll discuss later in this chapter.

All the above-described components — the keyboard, video screen, core computer (CPU, RAM and ROM), and magnetic media — can come individually packaged, can be combined in any of several combinations, or may arrive all in one unit. Often the keyboard and video screen are combined to form a terminal. (Having a detachable keyboard is *highly* desirable for serious word processing applications. We'll discuss the reasons for that in Chapter Twelve: **Selecting a Word Processing Computer.**) The core computer and disk drives are often combined in one box. Sometimes the core computer is hidden inside the terminal and the disk drives are in a box off to one side. Most often these days core computer, keyboard, video screen and disk drives come packaged all together in what looks like a television/typewriter with slots.

The last piece of equipment, which is almost always separate from the other components, is the **printer.** The printer does just what its name implies: it prints. It does this with great speed, far faster than human typing in most cases.

There are two kinds of printers, **dot matrix** and **letter quality**. Dot matrix printers form their letters by using dots, much like those signs on banks that tell you the time and the temperature. The dots are smaller than the light bulbs on those signs, but the effect is the same: the information is communicated efficiently, but far from elegantly.

```
This is a sample of dot matrix printing.
You will notice that the text is
perfectly readable, but the
printing is not as dignified as one
might require for business
correspondence or grant application.
```

```
Dot matrix printers can be set to go
over each line twice, which slows the
printing speed but improves the quality
of the type. This is an example of
double-running a dot matrix printer.
While an improvement, it is still not
worth writing home about. (It's good
enough to write home with but not
about.)
```

Letter quality printers use a ribbon and some sort of typing element to make a solid impression of each letter. The letters are printed, one after another, just as in typing, and it's difficult to tell the difference between a letter typed by a first-rate electric typewriter and a first-rate letter quality printer; hence, letter quality.

Dot matrix printers cost less to buy and print pages faster. Letter quality printers cost more to buy and print pages more slowly. The quality of a page printed on a letter quality printer is far superior to the quality of a page printed on a dot matrix printer.

So there we have the basic components of a personal computer. But what it is not yet is a word processor. To use all this equipment to process words, one key element must be added: a word processing **program**.

A program is to a computer what a record is to a phonograph. (Didn't you used to love those tests in school?

"The sun is to the moon as a _____ is to an artichoke.")
Without records, all the machinery that makes up a phonograph is useless. Without programs all the electronic circuitry and typewriter/televisions and magnetic media that make up a computer is likewise useless. In the hi-fi business, speakers and turntables and amplifiers are all known as hardware. Records are known as software. In Computerese, the computer and its peripherals are called hardware, programs are called **software**. You play a record; you **run** a program.

Whatever you want to do with a computer requires a program. It's the plan, the guide, the instructions and the rules that tell the various parts of the computer what to do when. If you want to balance your checkbook you run a checkbook program. If you want to play blackjack you run a blackjack program. If you want to write anything from a letter to a book, you run a word processing program.

A personal computer, then, with a word processing program, becomes a word processor.

Here we have an early personal computer on the left and an early word processor on the right. It's hard to believe that no one thought of putting the two together until the last quarter of the Twentieth Century

To review, the six main components of a personal computing system to be used for word processing are:

The Main Computer. This is made up of a Central Processing Unit (CPU), and two kinds of memory, Random Access Memory (RAM) and Read Only Memory (ROM). The CPU is smart, but has little memory. RAM and ROM have lots of memory, but are not very smart. Together they make a very happy triple. RAM is also known as user programmable memory.

The Video Screen. This looks like a television screen, in fact it *is* a television screen, but rather than tuning-in *Three's Company*, the screen displays letters, words, sentences and paragraphs. *(Three's Company* is being acted out in the main computer by CPU, ROM and RAM.)

The Keyboard. This looks like a typewriter keyboard, with a few extra keys added. The keyboard and video screen usually come in one unit, referred to as a **terminal.**

Disk Drives. Disk drives drive disks, also known as floppy disks or mini-disks. Disks are 5¼ or 8-inch circles of flexible plastic that store information. The disk drives record information onto disks, known as **writing**, and play information back, known as **reading**.

Printer. The printer does just that, it prints information onto paper. There are two kinds of printers: dot matrix, which forms letters using little dots; and letter quality, which types letters one at a time, much like an electric typewriter.

Program. All of the above machinery, known as **hardware**, would be for naught if it were not for programs, or **software**. Programs tell the computer what to do, when to do it, and how to do it. The variable that makes one computer an accounts receivable computer and makes an identical computer a word processing computer is the program. Programs are to computers what records are to phonographs.

In the next chapter we'll look at word processing programs in detail.

Some early word processors required one to write directly on the video screen...

While others required the help of another person...

And many writers appreciated the help very, very much

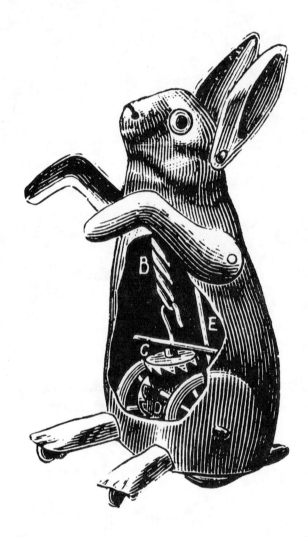

To help us better understand how computers operate, consider the mechanical rabbit. Rubber band (B) turns wheel (C) which moves gear (D) and pulls rod (E). That should certainly clarify the operation of personal computers

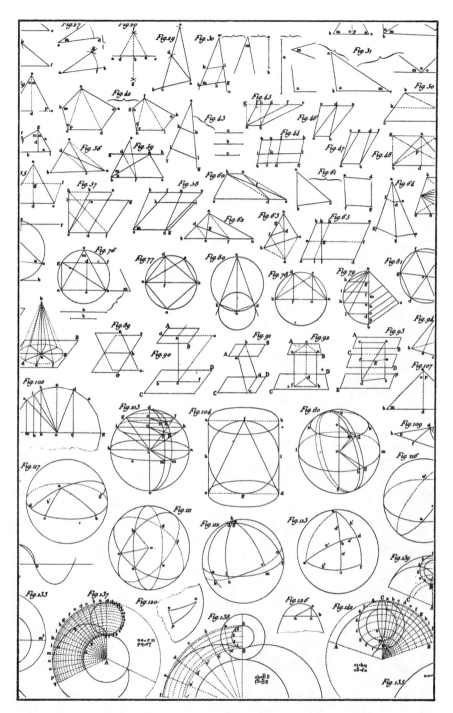

For those who find the "mechanical rabbit" explanation too elementary, here is a more detailed—although equally lucid—diagram

Chapter Three

The Wonders of
Word Processing

The Basics of Word Processing

Discussing word processing is like discussing Beethoven's Fifth Symphony. There are a great many recordings of this symphony, all different. Some are less different than others. The several versions done by the New York Philharmonic are going to be more similar to each other than the one done by the Omaha All Kazoo Band.

And so it is with word processing programs. There are about as many word processing programs as there are recordings of Beethoven's Fifth — maybe more. They're all different, but some are less different than others. The ones costing $500 are likely to be more similar to each other than are the ones costing $19.95.

All recordings of Beethoven's Fifth, from the Berliner Philharmonic to the Tijuana Symphony will begin with (we hope) "DA DA DA DUM." So, too, (we hope) do all word processing programs have some things in common. Let's look at those similarities, the basic features you can expect from any word processing program. Then we'll discuss the many variations, additions, and refinements that ingenious programmers have added in the past few years.

In explaining a basic word processing program, I'll use the typewriter for comparison. When you type on a typewriter, the words are transferred directly to the paper. When you type on a computer, the words appear on the video screen. Rather than ink on paper, you have written with electrons on phosphor. Ink on paper is hard to change; electrons on phosphor, easy.

If you make a mistake on a typewriter and catch it before putting too many characters between you and the mistake, you have several correcting options. The first is an eraser. Not recommended. The next is paint; little jars of white paint with brushes in them. You paint over the mistake, let it dry, and type over the paint. Similarly, there are little sheets of white carbon paper that will hide mistakes, in a fashion.

The ultimate solution to typing errors was the Wonder of the Age back in 1974: The IBM Correcting Selectric. On this machine you push a button, backspace to the mistake, retype the mistake, and a ribbon of flypaper comes out of the typewriter and magically lifts the offending characters right off the page! Why, this so thrilled typists throughout the country that there was a movement to give IBM Thursday of National Secretary's Week.

To make a correction on a word processor you press the "delete" button and watch it erase all that went before it, letter by letter until you release the button. You then type in, or "keyboard in" as they say in Computerese, whatever you would prefer to have in that space.

Let's say you've finished typing a page and it comes fresh and neat from the typewriter. You notice a sentence in the middle of the page that should not be there. Another sentence, that happens to be quite a bit longer than the sentence that should not be there, should be there. What do you have? A Moral Dilemma. A question worthy of Aristotle arises: "Is making this change that should be made worth retyping the whole page?" And if it's a long document, several pages long, and the pages have already been typed, the change would mean going onto another page, so the question becomes, "Is making this change that should be made worth retyping the whole document?"

If you own a word processor, you need never face that dilemma again. You will have to face other dilemmas, like how to pay for the word processor perhaps, but you will never face the to-retype-or-not-to-retype dilemma again. Whatever you're working on in word processing, from a wedding invitation to the great American novel, is known as a document. When you want to make a change in a document, you move the cursor to the point in the document where the change is to be made, and make it. A cursor is a little, blinking square that is the length and height of one letter —it tells you where you are in the document.

Taking words out, putting words in, correcting spelling, removing or adding literally pages of information can take place at any point in the document. The rest of the document adjusts accordingly, automatically, electronically. Change is easy because it's all done with electrons and electrons *love* to change. You could say it is one of their primary characteristics.

This ability to change what you want to change whenever you want to change it is the key to the value and growing popularity of word processing computers. With this feature, even the most basic word processing program can do more than the most expensive and sophisticated type-directly-onto-a-piece-of-paper typewriter.

After everything looks all right on the video screen, it comes time to print. Even the slowest printer types faster than all but the fastest typists, and printers can do it hour after hour after hour, 24 hours a day if necessary. The slower computer printers (converted IBM Selectrics, ironically enough) print at 15 characters per second (CPS). Figuring an average word to be seven letters long (that's just my figuring; heaven knows the length of an average word) that comes to 128.57 words per minute (WPM). The slower printers designed especially for computers print at 25 CPS or about 215 WPM; and the faster letter-perfect printers for computers travel at the remarkable rate of 55 CPS, which clocks in at around 470 words per minute. They print in both directions, from left to right and then, not to waste a return trip, from right to left. Many dot matrix printers go faster than that.

As you might gather, even if changes are desired after the document has been printed, making changes on the video screen and then printing a new document requires minimal time and effort. In fact, while doing word processing, working copies are printed all the time. The onus on retyping and re-retyping, and even re-re-retyping is gone. Push a few buttons and the printer clicks out a new copy in a matter of minutes.

The implication this has on personalized form letters is obvious. You can send out hundreds of letters, all saying the same thing, each looking hand typed, and the only thing you need to change each time is the name. And, Fellow writers: Freshly typed manuscripts are far more impressive than Xerox copies.

Those are the basics you can expect from any system that dares call itself a word processor. Although formidable, it's just the beginning.

Beyond the Basics of Word Processing

Some people require or desire a feature or two or twelve more than a basic word processing program provides. Who can blame them? After spending several thousand dollars on hardware, spending a few hundred more on better quality software that will turn their Volkswagen into a Mercedes is certainly understandable.

What follows is a guide to some of the features designers of word processing software have created. Each description will begin with the Computerese name for the feature.

File Length. File length determines how long a document can be. This is usually designated by the number of **K** or **Kilobytes**, each kilobyte being equal to 1024 **bytes**. A letter, number, character, or space is a **byte**. "20K" would be around 20,000 bytes, "240K" would be about 240,000 bytes, etc. If you're wondering what the relationship between a kilobyte and the written word is, a double-spaced, typewritten, 8½ x 11 sheet of paper with generous margins contains about 2,000 bytes, or 2K. Some less expensive word processing programs can handle only one or two pages of text at a time. (Of course, longer documents can be done one page at a time, just like on a typewriter.) The finest word processing software limits the size of the document to "disk capacity," meaning that, however many K the disk is capable of holding, that is the maximum length of the document.

Word Wrap. This means that when you reach the end of the line (meaning right-hand margin, not major life crisis), the next word will begin the next line automatically.

This may take some getting used to. If you're accustomed to a manual typewriter, you may find your left hand moving suddenly upwards and slapping the side of the video screen at the end of each line. Once you've become adjusted to word wrap, however, it's delightful. No more listening for the little bell. No more looking up to see how much room is left on a line. No more wondering if the next word will fit before the carriage stops dead. No more margin releases. Just type, type, type. The only time you'd use the carriage return is to begin a new paragraph or when you want the line to end before the right margin, such as in list making or poetry writing.

File Insertion. Each disk has many files. A file can be anywhere from one letter in length to the maximum length permitted by the word processing program. If you were typing along on file A, and you wanted to add the contents of files B, C, and D to file A, with the push of a few buttons it would be done.

Using file insertion you could create files of frequently used paragraphs or phrases and have them added to the text in a matter of seconds. This is great for correspondence or contracts. I have my name and address in a file marked AD and my name, address and phone number in a file marked ADP. When I come to the end of a letter and want to add my name and address I type two letters — a code to let the computer know that I want to "read" a file into my text — and then type AD. If I wanted to include my phone number I would type ADP. Zip. There it is.

Block Move. A block is a group of words that are all together in a bunch. I guess if you drew straight lines around a chosen bit of text on a printed page it would look like a block. I don't know. The logic of those three people who sat up until four in the morning making up these terms escapes me. At any rate, if you've ever written a paragraph and then wished it were in another part of the document, you will appreciate block moves.

All you'd need do is mark the beginning of the block, the end of the block, move the cursor to where you'd like that block to go, and within seconds the block has moved into its new neighborhood feeling very much at home. There are other good things you can do with blocks:

Copy Blocks, which lets you make a copy of the block, so that the original block stays where it is, but an identical copy can be written into another part of the document.

You can also copy a block onto another file. Let's say you're typing along and discover that you have written a paragraph that you will want to use again in other documents. You can copy it onto a new file, naming it whatever you like, and move on. The next time you need that paragraph you can use file insertion and read it into the text. All this moving around of blocks, by the way, is known as "text manipulation."

Global Search. Although this sounds like something James Bond might request ("We'll find him, sir. I'll have a global search run on him right away"), global search in word processing is far less dramatic, although equally exciting. Global search will find anything, at any point in your document, in a matter of seconds.

Let's say you have a very long document and you want to return to the section in which you were rhapsodizing about clouds. You would simply type the word "cloud" into global search and the computer would find and display the first time you used that word. If that wasn't quite the section you wanted, with the push of a button the computer would move to the point in your document where "cloud" was used for the second time, and so on.

Search and Replace. This not only finds any word or character in the document, it will change that word or character to any other word or character. If you've written a letter to Michael, using his name throughout the letter, and now you want to send the same letter to Mary, all you do is have the computer find each occurrence of "Michael" and change it to "Mary." In a few seconds the letter will be personalized to Mary.

Another use for search and replace is to save typing. Let's suppose you're doing a very long report on the heterobasidiomycetes (a subclass of fungi, for the two or three out there who didn't know. You know who you are.) Now, writing as you would be on heterobasidiomycetes, you would no doubt have to mention the word heterobasidiomycetes quite often. You might not want to type out heterobasidiomycetes as many times as you'd be using heterobasidiomycetes, and you may, in fact, after awhile, find yourself avoiding the word heterobasidiomycetes altogether. Now, rather than type out the word heterobasidiomycetes each time, with search and replace all you would have to do is use an abbreviation, say "H" each time you wanted to use heterobasidiomycetes. When finished you would simply have search and replace find all occurrences of "H" and replace them with "heterobasidiomycetes." In this way your report, your fingers, and your sanity are saved by search and replace.

Dictionary. (Also known as Proofreader or Spell Check or something along those lines.) This checks every word in your document against a list of correctly spelled words. These lists of correctly spelled words range from 10,000 to 45,000 words. If a word in your document does not match a word in the word list, it means that either the word is misspelled or the word is correctly spelled but not located in the program's list of words.

The dictionary feature will make a list of the unmatched words for you to examine. If they are correctly spelled they can be added to the dictionary. All future checks will include those words. If they are incorrectly spelled they are automatically marked in the text and found using global search. (A "*" for example, is placed by the program before each misspelled word. You have global search find all incidences of the symbol "*" and, one by one, the misspelled words will present themselves for correction.) Incorrect spellings, by the way, include most typographical errors. This feature is great for ferreting out typing mistakes, the ones usually discovered *after* the letter is sent.

Most often this feature will not be found as part of a word processing program, but can be purchased as a separate program and used with whatever word processing software you own. The best dictionary programs will look up the correct spelling for a word, even if you don't know how it's spelled. You type in how you think it's spelled and, nine times out of ten, it will come up with the correct spelling. (The next chapter, **The Curse of Noah Webster** looks at one of these dictionary programs in greater detail.)

Centering. The computer will automatically center any word or group of words between the left and right margins. Great for headings, titles, addresses, invitations, poetry, and the like.

Page Display. This will display on the video screen where the page breaks will be when the document is printed. It helps avoid the last three words of a paragraph beginning a new page.

Automatic Pagination. The page numbers will automatically be printed at the bottom, top, left, or right side of every page. Like most features, this one can be "switched off" so that no page numbers print.

Screen Oriented. Programs that are screen oriented mean that what you see on the video screen is what you'll get on the printed page. If you want justified right margins, they will be displayed that way on the screen. If you make a change, that change is reflected instantly on the screen in both the content of the words and the format the words are in.

Word processing programs that are not screen oriented are known as **character oriented.** This means that you see all the words displayed in the order, but not necessarily in the format, that they will be printed. Some people don't mind this. As long as one word follows another as written and the new paragraphs begin when requested, that's all that matters. Others will want to see what they're working on, in the form it will be printed, as they go.

Justification. No, this is not a list of good excuses for why you spent so much money on a fancy typewriter. This means that the right margin is straight and even, just like the left. Most books, newspapers and magazines use justified right and left margins, also known as "flush right" and "flush left."

Studies have shown, however, that while perfectly justified right and left margins look more impressive on a printed page, unjustified ("ragged") right margins are easier to read. Moral: If you want to impress, turn the justification on. If you want to communicate, turn it off. (And you can see where *this* book stands!)

Justification is done by expanding shorter lines. This expansion is done by adding spaces. If little itsy-bitsy-teeny-tiny spaces are added between letters, this is known as **microspacing.**

Proportional Spacing. A typewriter allots the same amount of space for each letter, so that a capital "W" is the same width as a small "i." Proportional spacing prints the "W" wider than an "a" and an "a" wider than an "i." Most books and magazines print with proportional spacing. Proportional spacing produces printed copy that is as close as you can get to professional typesetting. This requires, of course, not only the appropriate software but also one of the better letter quality printers.

While we're on the subject of printers, why don't we wind up this review of word processing capabilities with some of the many printing enhancements that are available when a first-rate printer and top-quality word processing program combine. In fact, let's switch from professional phototypesetting to a letter quality word processing printer.

Underlining. We all know what underlining is. At least I <u>hope</u> we all know what underlining is. Underlining is when you draw a line <u>under</u> something. The words "hope" and "under" were <u>underlined,</u> as was the word "underlined." (Do you see how boring this book must be to anyone who knows a lot about word processing?)

Double Strike. This means that every character is typed twice. It gives a darker, more solid impression and would stand out on a page, but not quite as blatantly as boldface. It is very useful for preparing copy that is later to be printed.

Boldface. Here, too, each character is typed twice, but the second impression is slightly to one side of the first. The "slightly" is very slight, so that the two impressions overlap and form one dark, solid character.

Pitch Changes. This refers to how many characters there are per inch. The pitches we're most accustomed to are pica, which is ten characters per inch, and elite, twelve characters per inch. The better programs and printers allow you to change from one to another, at any point, without interrupting the printing. At least one system can print as few as four characters per inch, and as many as thirty. Thirty characters per inch. As my father would say, "Can you feature that?" Well, all right, I will feature that. Here is what "Come live with me and be my love and we will all the pleasures prove" looks like at thirty characters per inch:

Come live with me and be my love and we will all the pleasures prove.

Subscript and **Superscript.** These functions put the words, characters or numbers slightly below or slightly above the line they are printed on. It's useful when writing H_2O

51

(the "2" is in subscript) or $E=MC^2$ (the "2" is in superscript.)

Kerning. Kerning is a term from printing that refers to the spacing between letters. Some word processing software allows the movement of a single letter to the right or to the left in infinitesimal increments.

Overprinting. This allows you to print one character over another. It's useful in foreign languages, when you want to put the "`" over the "e" in "olè" or if you want to create your own characters, as someone did when he combined the "?" with the "!" and came up with "‽". It's called an interrobang and it's used to punctuate sentences such as "You're what‽" or "You're going where‽" or "You just bought a word processing what‽"

Strikeout. For the life of me I cannot see the point of strikeout. All it does is put little dashes (-----) over whatever you've written and prints it that way. You pay all this money for a word processing machine so that there will never have to be any more strikeouts or erasures or white carbon paper or white paint all over your documents and then they include a special way of making them look bad. I don't know. The only possible use I can come up with is to make typewriter-like mistakes so that no one will know you have a word processing machine and nobody will want to come over and use it. That's all I can figure. (I am told this has some value in a law office. A great many unusual things do.)

The text above is an example of proportionally spaced printing on a word processor. The text you are reading now is an example of nonproportional (regular) spacing. With regular spacing, each letter is allowed the same amount of room no matter how wide or narrow it might be. This is standard for typewriters. The type faces are designed, in fact, so that an "i" is wider than it might normally be and an "M" is narrower.

This paragraph and the one just above are also set with right-and-left justified margins (obviously) using microspacing. The spaces necessary to extend shorter lines to the right margin are added in between each letter rather than in between each word.

The look of a printed document is also affected by the choice of type styles, and how those type styles are manipulated. This is the same typeface as the previous two paragraphs, but the pitch was changed from 10 to 12 pitch. In this way the same print wheel gives different results.

Print wheels can be changed, of course, and a wide variety of type styles is available. We just switched from Courier to Times Roman. The proportional spacing above was printed in Emperor. Some word processing programs allow for print wheel changes *within* sentences. This allows one to *italicize* words by changing type wheels. **Boldface** does not require changing type wheels since it is done **automatically** by the printer and the word processing program.

For most correspondence you'll want people to think it was typed on a regular (albeit expensive electric) typewriter. You'll probably want to turn the right justification off. If you send out left-and-right justified letters people will know you have a word processor and suspect form paragraphs ——or worse——form letters. To maintain the illusion, you can print correspondence ragged right.

———————————————◇◇◇◇◇———————————————

This chapter has exhausted only you and me. It has far from exhausted all the features currently available on word processing programs, and more are coming every day. Whatever your personal needs involving the processing of words, the chances are good that the program exists that will make your task a whole lot easier. If they can help me spell, they can do anything.

Chapter Four

The Curse of Noah Webster

I have always had a fondness for Thomas Jefferson. Anyone who wrote the Declaration of Independence and said, "I have nothing but contempt for anyone who can spell a word only one way," can't be all bad. I will not be spending much time on the Declaration of Independence in this chapter, but I have a feeling that I will be discussing the subject of spelling a great deal.

I am an awful speller. I am so bad that I don't even know when a word is spelled correctly. Ninety percent of the words I take the time to look up (and I do mean time: I'm lousy at alphabetical order, too) are right in the first place. It's discouraging. Hence, one of the deciding factors in my purchase of a computer with word processing capabilities was the flurry of programs promising to forever end the Curse of Noah Webster. (He's the one who started it all, you know. He's the one who came along 198 years ago and gave Americans only one way to spell a word. The right way. His way.)

In my research I came across a bit of dictionary software that not only does more than any of the others I've used or read about, but costs less. Far less.

The WORD retails for $75. (Spellguard, the trade name for another popular spelling-correction program, costs $295. Others run in the $200-250 range.) "The first question people ask me," says the creator of The WORD, Wayne Holder, "is 'What's wrong with it? Why is it so cheap?'" Thus far I've found nothing "wrong," and a good deal right, with it.

I will use a description of The WORD's several programs as the basis for this chapter. Not only will it tell you what is available in dictionary software today, but it will show you how special features can be added to whatever word processing program you decide upon.

The dictionary in The WORD is massive, more than 45,000 words. The dictionary is compressed, allowing that many words, plus all other programs and commands, to fit into less than 154K of disk space. (The dictionary uses 136K of that.)

The WORD will do what all the other "dictionary" programs will do, namely check each word in the text against the correctly spelled words in the dictionary; list words that do not match (indicating misspellings, typos, uncommon proper names, jargon or technical terms); and then, after the option to edit the list, mark the mismatched words in the text for correction.

The latest edition of The WORD (version 2.0) uses a feature called REVIEW. Each of the mismatched words appears, one by one, and with a single keystroke you can either mark the misspelled word in the text for later correction; add the word, if correctly spelled, to the dictionary so that the word will never appear on a mismatched word list again; add the correctly spelled word to a special dictionary that will only be checked upon request; or delete the word from the mismatch list altogether.

What if you accidentally delete a word that should have been added to the dictionary, or add a word to the dictionary that should have been marked as a misspelling? Review is very forgiving. You simply back up and reroute the word to its desired location. (If you have a version of The WORD prior to 2.0, OASIS will update it for only $10.)

To find the correct spelling for the words that are misspelled, The WORD uses a program descriptively entitled LOOKUP. LOOKUP is a tool that, from my point of view, is worth far more than $75 all by itself. One simply types "LOOKUP" and the way one *thinks* the word should be spelled, and LOOKUP will, nine times out of ten, find the correct spelling. I misspelled twelve words in the writing of this chapter and LOOKUP found the acceptable-to-Mr.-Webster spelling for eleven of them.

It does this, I am told, by "correcting" the word in a great many ways, using the four most common mistakes in spelling, checking these "corrections" against the main dictionary, and listing the words that match. All this takes about ten seconds.

If I were to ask it to LOOKUP THIER, for example, The WORD would list THEIR, THIEF and TIER. I may be bad at spelling, but of the three I know the word I'm looking for is THEIR.

A problem in any spell-check program is homonyms. Homonyms are words that are pronounced the same but spelled differently, depending on their use: words like "stationary" and "stationery"; "their," "they're," and "there"; "to," "too," and "two." Take the sentence: "Their going two the stationary store, to." Although this sentence would sound all right if it were spoken, and although individual words are correctly spelled, because of each word's usage there are four misspellings in that sentence. "They're going to the stationery store, too." would be correct. Since dictionary programs can only check the spelling of words, and not their context in a sentence, homonyms are a problem.

The WORD offers a partial solution to this problem. The program has a file of 860 homonyms. You go through and remove the homonyms you know how to use correctly. The ones that remain are potential troublemakers for you, and The WORD will, upon request, mark these words in the text for closer review.

Another fascinating feature of The WORD, indispensable to crossword puzzle fanatics (who don't mind a little help) and writers who need to rhyme (who welcome all the help they can get), is FIND. Based upon the number of letters known, with "?" or "*" representing the letters unknown, FIND will find all the words that might fit the format you request. If, for example, you were doing a crossword puzzle and you needed a four-letter word that ended in "Q," all you'd need do is type "FIND ???Q" (each "?" represents one letter) and in less than a minute FIND would tell you that the word you're most likely looking for is "IRAQ."

If you were writing an "Ode To My Computer" and were seeking a melodic match for "terminal," all you'd do to find more than enough rhymes is enter "FIND *AL" ("*" represents any number of letters) and all words, of any length, ending in "AL" would come flooding forth (as a poet might say). This would give a nearly endless list of words. To tighten the rhyme you might want to remove just the first letter and enter "FIND *ERMINAL." This yields only one possibility, GERMINAL. So you might want to loosen the rhyme a bit and leave off the first syllable, entering "FIND *MINAL." This brings forth from the depths of iron oxide such gems as CRIMINAL, NOMINAL and SEMINAL.

Two more great tools for the writer included in The

WORD are Wordcount (WC) and Word Frequency (WORD-FREQ). There are 2,099 words in this chapter. It took Wordcount about three seconds to give me that information. (Can you imagine how long it would have taken me to give me that information?) However, there are only 611 unique words. That is, I used 611 words, and by repeating some, came up with a 2,099-word chapter. Which words were repeated, and how many times each? That's where Word Frequency comes in.

Word Frequency tells how many times each word in the document was used, and will list them either in descending order of usage or alphabetically. The Top Ten words in this chapter are: **THE** (with a whopping 165 occurrences), **WORD** (with 76), **AND** edged out **A** (with 55 and 54 respectively), **IN** (53), **OF** (51), **TO** (47), **FOR** (35), **IS** (30) and, egomaniac that I am, I used **I** 29 times. Of the 611 unique words, 349 of them were used only once.

So, I used 611 words, 349 only once, repeated 262 of them as many as 165 times each to form a 2,099-word chapter. Now where else in the world could I come up with that information?

DICTSORT (Dictionary Sorter) is a program that will put any group of words in alphabetical order within seconds. If it puts one index of one book in order, it's paid for itself. Also great for mailing lists, record collections (mine is: Popular, alphabetical by artist; Classical, alphabetical by composer), or, if you're more like Daniel Webster than Noah Webster, it will put your book of "Alternative Spellings for Free Americans" in perfect order faster than you can say, "Life, liberty and the pursuit of happiness."

Each 5¼-inch disk on my word processing computer will hold about 340K of information. I've combined The WORD with WordStar (a word processing program described in Chapter Thirteen), along with a few of my own boilerplate paragraphs, on one disk and I still have 80K to spare. I use this disk for correspondence, articles, or short chapters. I enter text, edit, correct spelling, and print, all without changing drives. I then copy the file onto an appropriate storage disk, erase the original, and have 80K again for my next project.

The WORD is fast. With my system, spelling is checked on shorter documents in under a minute. I clocked an 8,382 word document at one minute and nineteen seconds, a 10,535 word document in one minute and forty-nine seconds. It would take me an hour to read, much less proofread, a 10,535 word document!

The 42-page manual is clear, friendly, and to the point. It includes all you'll need to know to be working The WORD within an hour. (Maybe less for you: I'm as bad at reading as I am at spelling.)

I can heartily recommend any of the several programs contained in The WORD for the $75 price; and when they're all together, in one package, at that same price, well, it's one of the great software bargains around.

Some people can't leave well enough alone. Wayne Holder seems to be one of these people. Not content with a perfectly good spell-check program, he had to go and improve it. The result is The WORD Plus. If you were happy with The WORD, you'll be ecstatic with The WORD Plus.

The WORD Plus is **menu driven**. A menu in personal computing is the same as a menu in a restaurant: It lists all that's available. Menu driven also means that the programs, or portions of the programs, will be presented in a logical order for selection. In a restaurant this logical order might be appetizer, soup, salad, main course, dessert.

In a spell-check program, the first logical question would be, "Which file would you like checked?" This is The WORD Plus's first question. One types in the name of the file and hits the return key. The WORD Plus checks the file for misspellings, tells you how many there are, and then automatically goes into the REVIEW program.

As described earlier in this chapter, the REVIEW program presents words not found in the 45,000-word dictionary one at a time for, well, review.

One can delete the word from the misspelled list, add the word to the dictionary, or mark the word in the text. With The WORD Plus, one has several other choices. One can, for example, ask for the context in which the word appeared. If the misspelled word is "ands," should it have been "and," "ends," "sands," or one of several other possible words? Looking at the misspelled word alone, it's hard to tell. With the press of one button (the V key for "View"), The WORD Plus displays the line from the original text in which the word appears.

After discovering that the word should be "and," one pushes the C key (for "correct") and types "AND." The WORD Plus will, wonder of wonders, change "ands" to "and" in the text. No need to mark the word with an asterisk and return to the text and change it; the correction takes place automatically.

The WORD Plus incorporates the LOOKUP feature in REVIEW. Simply push L and within a few seconds (less than five on my computer), several possible correct spellings for the misspelled word are listed. With two keystrokes the correct word is noted and the acceptable-to-Mr.-Webster spelling automatically replaces the misspelled word in the text.

Two features, not directly connected to spelling correction, but helpful in the processing of words, are a part of The WORD Plus. The first is HYPHEN. As the names implies, this program will either suggest possible hyphenations for individual words, or place "soft hyphens" in all the words in a given text. Soft hyphens are hyphens that print as hyphens only when they fall at the end of a line, otherwise the words print whole without hyphenation. This is invaluable in documents with narrow margins, long words, or both.

The second, almost for fun, is called ANAGRAM. This will find anagrams for any word or collection of letters — provided, of course, that the anagrams to be found are listed in the 45,000-word dictionary. (An anagram of ANIMAL is MANILA, for example. Anagrams for SAINT include STAIN and SATIN.)

Beyond solving word-scramble puzzles and finding character names that subconsciously hint at personality traits, ANAGRAM will find words based upon *sounds*.

Let's say you were writing a story and wanted to set the mood with ooo sounds, like soothing or smooth. One would simply type in "ANAGRAM OO???" and all five-letter words with two Os would appear — a long list with BLOOM,

MOONS and ROMEO among them. How about all six letter words with three Os? Type "ANAGRAM OOO???" and one discovers such beautiful words as COCOON, ROCOCO and COMORO (a group of Islands in the Mozambique Channel).

If you wanted to find some buzz words, I mean real buzz words, words with some zip and pizzazz to them, you could type in "ANAGRAM ZZ???" and be pelted with DIZZY, FRIZZ and JAZZY. Harder sounding words? Let's try "ANAGRAM KK???." We're assaulted with KHAKI, KINKY and our old friend KODAK.

The WORD Plus sells for $150, half as much as the best-selling spell-check program, although The WORD Plus does much, much more. Those who own The WORD can upgrade to The WORD Plus for $75.

The WORD Plus approaches perfection in spell-check programs; it certainly is the state of the art. But some people can leave neither perfection nor the state of the art alone....

(to be continued.)

This early word processor required two adults and a small child to operate. The keyboard is left, video screen in the center, printer on the right.

PART II

The Uses of
Word Processing Computers

When an operator tells you that she uses the

Remington

she stands up a little straighter.

She knows as well as you do that her choice of the Recognized Leader among Typewriters is a fine recommendation-- one which raises her in your estimation.

Remington Typewriter Company

(Incorporated)

New York and Everywhere

Chapter Five

Word Processing
in The Office

**What Would Happen If I Traded In
My Selectric for a Computer?**

Ladies and gentlemen, welcome to yet another edition of *Peter Predicts*. On this show I deal with the future for, as the Great Criswell has said, the future is where you and I are going to spend the rest of our lives.

I see the Prediction of the Day coming to me from the clouded mists of the future. Today's prediction is: By 1990, every Selectric in every office in America will be replaced by a word processing computer. I see small business machine dealers very upset, because their vast inventory of previously owned Selectrics has depreciated by two-thirds. I see IBM, happy as always, because their $1,000 Selectrics are being replaced by their $4,000 IBM Personal Computers. I see business people angry because they waited too long to "go word processing," and now the trade-in value of their Selectric has dropped to a level slightly higher than the value of a fifty-pound-all-mechanical-Burroughs-Calculating-Machine-circa-1965. I see...I see...the screen of my crystal video display screen is clouding. That's all for today.

Okay, enough of the future and *Peter Predicts*. Let's return to the present and *Peter Reports*. This chapter will answer the office manager's burning question, "What can a personal computer, with a letter-quality printer, running a word processing program, do for my office?" And, to the secretary in that office, the question answered will be, "What would happen if I traded in my Selectric for a word processing computer?" ("Selectric" in this chapter will represent any expensive electric typewriter.)

Before we begin, let me apologize for the sexist language it was necessary to use in this chapter. The perpetration of the stereotype that the boss is a man and referred to as "he" and the secretary is a woman and referred to as "she" was necessary in this chapter. There were too many sentences that read, "He or she asked his or her secretary to type his or her letter on his or her typewriter." It was awkward and unclear. "He asked her to type his letter on her typewriter" may be full of sexist assumptions, but it does communicate. Please feel free to switch around in your mind any "he" that refers to a boss or "she" that refers to a secretary.

This chapter will not deal with multi-user systems, in which one computer connects an entire office with dozens of terminals. Although most of the features discussed in this chapter would apply to multi-user systems, the installation and use of a multi-user system is beyond the scope of this book.

Just because a company is large, however, is no reason to automatically assume that one big computer with lots of terminals is the way to go. In some situations it is, and in others, buying a word processing computer for every person currently using a Selectric might prove more cost effective. (This and the next several paragraphs are obviously directed at office managers of large corporations, and I must use terms like "cost effective" to keep their attention.) Below are a few of the reasons why individual word processing computers might be better than one large computer with many terminals.

1. It takes a long time, a lot of money, and an unbearable amount of expert consultation to decide which large computer to buy. Further, it is often difficult to justify the expense of buying a large computer for word processing alone. Higher-ups will say, "Well, we already have a computer. Let's use that one." The computer in the data-processing department may be ill-suited for word processing or may be too small to add a dozen extra terminals. And how do you prove a large word processing computer will do any good? This takes yet another study, and another study takes more time and more money. And on and on and on.

Buying a personal computer or two, and having them replace a Selectric or two, is not as difficult. Within six months you'll have information from within your own company on how they are doing. If the results are positive, then several more machines can be added. Six months later, if the results are still favorable, you can get a word processing computer for everyone. It'll take a year, but that will be less time than most corporations spend researching and buying a large computer.

2. There is a fear of computers among some office workers. In starting slowly, you can give word processors to those who are anxious to have them. They will use them well, the fearful will learn that there is nothing to fear, and within a brief period of time the formerly frightened will be

demanding computers of their own.

3. How often have you heard the phrase "Our computer is down?" Like most of us, computers do "get down" from time to time. If twenty people are dependent upon one computer for all their word processing needs, you can imagine what happens when the computer stops working. If, however, you have twenty separate computers and one breaks, it's hardly noticed. In larger corporations, having an extra word processing computer "in reserve" would be a justifiable — if not intelligent — expense.

4. Since a word processing computer is nothing more than a small computer programed for word processing, it is easy to run other programs. One executive, for example, might need to have accurate stock market quotations. His secretary could have her computer linked to one of the information services that provide up-to-the-minute stock market information. For another executive, financial projections using an "electronic worksheet" program might prove invaluable. A third might need ongoing airline information, a fourth might use electronic mail, and so on.

Rather than having a terminal attached to an inflexible large computer, you have the advantages of many small computers and the flexibility they offer.

5. If it happens all at once, the transition from individual typewriters to large computer can be a nightmare. The addition of individual word processors can take place gradually, over a period of time, and the overall workflow of the office need not be disturbed.

6. Twenty personal computers, complete with printers and word processing software would, at $7,000 per computer, cost $140,000. You can *easily* spend that much researching, purchasing, and programming a large, twenty-terminal computer.

There are situations in which it is far more economical to buy one large computer. I mention the advantages of individual word processing computers because, if you call in a word processing expert who has spent the last ten years installing nothing but large-scale word processing operations, it is doubtful that he or she will mention any of the above. It is in fact possible that the expert might not even *know* any of the above. Personal computers have been around for a very few years. Many of the Big Computer Experts continue to look upon them as toys.

This chapter will also not tell you how to turn your typing pool into an electronic sweatshop. Some businesses have programmed their word processors to count the number of key strokes per hour each keyboard operator makes. This is noted in a daily report, and each day the operator is expected to type faster and faster. I see this as tyranny of the worst sort, and a glowing example of using the remarkable powers of computers to enslave rather than to free.

What we will be looking at, then, is what would happen if that large, expensive, electric typewriter — be it the only one in an office, or one of several hundred — were replaced by a slightly larger, electric, more expensive word processing computer.

Let's look at the various tasks a typewriter is most often used for in an office, and see how a word processing computer would handle the same tasks.

Certainly one of the primary uses for a typewriter in the office is correspondence: letters, notes, memos and the like. It would seem, from superficial examination, that some kinds of correspondence would benefit from word processing and others would not. Form letters, or letters that might use boilerplate paragraphs, would obviously fall into the "it would benefit" category, whereas original correspondence, in which a letter is dictated and typed only once, would not. Let's see if the latter assumption is true.

To type an original letter on a typewriter, one puts a piece of paper in the typewriter, types, and takes the letter out of the typewriter. Simple. To type an original letter on a word processor, one must put a disk in the disk drive, create a file, type the letter (which would be displayed on the video screen), put a piece of paper in a printer, instruct the computer to print the letter, watch while the letter is printed, and remove the letter. Not as simple.

It would seem, then, that if most of the work done by a given secretary were original letters, a word processor could be a hindrance. But let's look a bit more closely at how an original letter is created.

Most original letters are dictated. The secretary types the letter from the notes she has taken, and submits the letter for a signature. If there's a single typo or misspelling (bosses seem to *enjoy* finding mistakes, don't they?), then the entire letter must be retyped. If typos are found in the retyped letter it must be typed again, etc., etc. If the letter is free from secretarial error, the boss, seeing his thoughts immortalized on paper for the first time, will no doubt begin making changes. Even a simple "add this" or "take that out" means only one thing to the secretary: "retype the whole thing."

The word "retype" is seldom mentioned in a word processed office, just as the phrase "crank it up" has fallen into disuse around automobile circles since the advent of the electric starter. The phrases linger for nostalgia's sake more than anything else, I think; car batteries are rated for their "cold cranking" abilities, and a boss in a word-processing office will occasionally say, "Would you retype this?" But what he means, and what the secretary hears, is, "Would you make these changes and print a new copy?"

Making changes is fast and easy. Simply call the file up on the video screen, remove what is unwanted, add what is wanted, and print the results. Fast letter-quality printers turn out freshly printed documents at the rate of a page per minute.

Even if no changes are made, the speed at which a spell-check program can ferret out spelling and typing errors make a word processor more than earn its keep.

Then we come into the areas of correspondence at which word processors truly shine: boilerplate paragraphs and form letters. Most businesses have paragraphs, even whole letters, that repeat themselves day after day after day. "Thank you for inquiring about our new Wonder Widget...." "We certainly hope you will enjoy your new Wonder Widget...." "All of us are prostrate with grief that your new Wonder Widget did not live up to your expectations...." And so on. With a word processor, these boilerplate paragraphs can be stored on a disk and added to the letter whenever necessary. Once added, they can be altered, added to, or shortened.

I have a boilerplate paragraph I use whenever I write a letter of complaint. I attempt to shame the company into not sending me a form letter response. I do this with a form paragraph. It reads:

> I am reminded of the man who wrote a letter to the Pullman Company back in the 1940s, complaining of bedbugs in his sleeping car. He received a very apologetic letter saying that this was the first they had ever heard of such a thing and that all the cars were being fumigated as a response to his letter. Along with this letter was enclosed, by mistake, the original letter of complaint the man had sent. Written by hand at the bottom of the letter was: "Send this SOB the bedbug letter." I certainly hope that I will not receive a "bedbug" letter from you.

I have this paragraph in a file named "PULLMAN," and it takes but a few seconds to add it to the text of any letter or, in this case, book. To type it would take several minutes, and to find the original to type it from would no doubt take longer.

Names and addresses are typed and retyped in the course of a business day. A name and address is first found on the Rollodex, then typed at the top of the letter. Later, the same information will be typed once again on an envelope. With a word processor, a mailing list can be kept on a disk. In less than the time it takes to find a file on a Rollodex, the computer has not only found but added to your letter the name and address in question. When it comes time to print the envelope, a command or two from the keyboard takes care of it.

Form letters are well known to us all. The same thing needs to be said to fifty people, but each person must receive the information personally typed. A task of this kind in a Selectric office would sentence a normally cheerful, productive secretary to a day of drudgery and depression.

In a business I once ran we would hire various sales organizations to sell our wares, each organization having a dozen-or-so salespeople. Now, these were the people who would be selling our product for, in some cases, an entire state. I felt that a personalized letter welcoming them and telling them about the company seemed in order. This began as a two-page letter, but soon grew to five. Each time I hired a new sales organization my secretary would, understandably, grow pale and bored (boredom is hostility without enthusiasm). About the time that I thought it would be a good idea to thank every buyer who ordered from us with a personalized letter, she quit. The two events were no doubt related.

On a word processor, fifty personalized, one-page letters would take less than an hour. With an automatic sheet feeder (a device that attaches to the printer and feeds individual pieces of paper into the printer one sheet at a time), the operation would require minimal supervision.

Most programs permit the automatic insertion of the name or other information within the letter, so that, "I know you'll find Minnesota Wonder Widget Country, Jim!" in one letter automatically becomes, "I know you'll find Hawaii Wonder Widget Country, Carol!" in the next. In addition, each of the fifty letters would not require individual proof reading. Only the name and address would need verification; the balance would be letter-perfect.

Most of the other office tasks requiring a typewriter are extensions of the letter, and the contributions made by a word processing computer would be very much the same.

Reports, for example, are subject to many revisions before the final draft is approved. The same report may be retyped a dozen times before it is deemed suitable for circulation. The absence of retyping word processing brings to letters, it brings with an even greater sigh of relief to reports.

On larger documents, some of word processing's other features are useful: the freedom to move a paragraph from one part of the document to another in a matter of seconds, for example, or the ability to find all occurrences of a word or phrase and change it to a different word or phrase. Using right-justified margins adds a professional look, and if you use proportional spacing they'll think you sent it out to be typeset.

On long documents, the computer's ability to find typos and misspellings is particularly valuable. The longer the document, the harder it becomes to find mistakes. As the operating manual for The WORD points out, "Studies have shown that in documents longer than 20 pages, most people fail to find more than 50% of the misspelled words." A good spell-check program won't miss a one.

Once perfect, in what form should the report be circulated? Who gets original typed copies and who gets Xerox facsimiles? With a word processor, nearly everyone can receive a personally typed copy.

Having the report on a disk can become quite valuable. You may wish to quote from it; it could form the backbone of a great many well-written letters. With only minor changes, a report to the President can become a report to the Board of Directors and with a few more changes a newsletter for the sales force is born.

Speaking of newsletters, we might as well speak about newsletters. Newsletters are the duty of some secretaries, and word processors make organizing them relatively easy. To put together, for example, an inspirational message from "the boss," simply go through some recent correspondence (all neatly stored on disks), select a few timeless excerpts, arrange them in a logical order and there you have it. No need to retype any of these gems. Just copy them from the files on which they are stored. You can "cut and paste" electronically, some word processing programs letting you set the type with right-and left-justified margins around spaces for photographs or drawings. Print a copy, add photos and drawings, and it's ready for the printer or the Xerox machine.

THE REMINGTON
Perfected Type-Writer.

Employment for Girls! Easy, genteel, profitable.

Copying at home, or *writing in Business Offices.* Hundreds in such positions, in all parts of the country are earning from 8 to 20 dollars per week. See article on page 467, issue of Dec. 8, of this paper. Send for circular. **E. REMINGTON & SONS,** 281 & 283 Broadway, New York.

[1882]

And now for the bad news (or, if you have a deep emotional attachment to your Selectric, the good news): What typewriters do better than word processors. The list is small. Come to think of it, it's not even a list; it's just one thing. What Selectrics do better than word processors: Fill in blanks. When you type on a word processor, the text is displayed on a screen first and printed on paper later, therefore it's difficult to tell precisely on which line what typing will fall. With a Selectric, you position the ball above the line in question and type away.

It is not impossible to fill out forms with most word processors. CP/M based systems (CP/M is a disk operating system we'll discuss in Chapter Twelve) have a simple command that turns the keyboard/printer into a mock-Selectric. Position the form in the printer, then use the keyboard to type the information. One must be careful, though: unlike a correcting Selectric, there is no ribbon of fly paper to magically lift your mistakes from the paper. If you make a mistake it's back to Correctype.

It is because of forms, and one-time labels, that people keep a Selectric or small electric typewriter around the word processed office. It depends on the number and kind of forms and labels needed.

Usually standard company forms can be filled out faster on the word processor once the operator knows the spatial relationship between the form and the screen. Sometimes a special program can be run that duplicates the forms of a company, and sometimes it's simply a matter of knowing that question 23 should be answered on line 42, column 12. Line and column information is usually displayed somewhere on the video screen, and getting to a certain line and column is easy.

So much for what a Selectric can do better than a word processor.

Let's look at a few of the random benefits gained by having a word processing computer around the office.

Earlier in this chapter I mentioned the ability to run programs other than word processing programs on the computer. The only difference between a word processing computer and an accounting computer is the software.

In an office in which one person is responsible for not only correspondence and reports but also invoicing and bookkeeping, a personal computer equipped with both word processing and accounting programs could easily double the effectiveness of this person.

In slightly larger offices, where billing and such is done by one person and correspondence is handled by another (the classic "this is my bookkeeper and this is my secretary" situation), it is sometimes possible to share one computer between two people. The bookkeeper gets it in the morning, the secretary in the afternoon or something like that.

If the need is so great that two terminals would be

required, my (rather radical I do admit) suggestion: Buy two computers. Most two-terminal set-ups, in which one person is doing word processing and the other is doing data processing, require a hard disk, and that adds enough to the

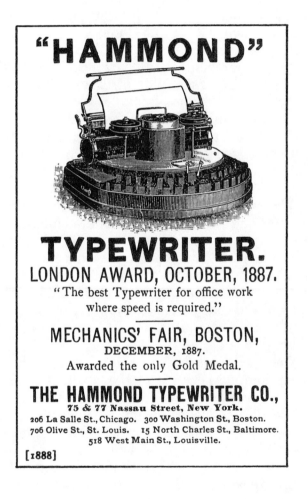

price that you might as well get two computers. Accounting will probably be happier with a dot-matrix printer anyway, so that saves $1,000, bringing the difference between buying one two-terminal hard disk computer or two one-terminal floppy disk computers within a couple thousand dollars.

The installation of a two-terminal computer is more elaborate and its operation more complicated. Further, if the accounting computer is down and the checks must go out, it's comforting to know that the secretary's word processing computer can be converted to an accounting computer in a matter of seconds — assuming you bought two identical computers, which is a very good idea.

In a larger office, one that has its own "dp" (data processing) department with its own computers, the ability to run the literally thousands of programs available for a CP/M system can be quite valuable. To list them would (and does) fill a book. Suffice it to say that whatever your business there are no doubt programs — from figuring the amortization of a mortgage to balancing the boss's personal checkbook— that will make the secretary's work not only easier, but more effective.

Whatever the office size, being able to use the computer to connect to one of the information data banks could benefit just about any business. The Source and CompuServe are two of the largest. Your computer connects to one of these data banks using a telephone and a device called a **modem**. You dial the local access number of the data bank, activate the modem, and your personal computer becomes a terminal for a very large computer that has access to an enormous amount of information.

You can research any subject; read the electronic edition of the *New York Times*, the *Los Angeles Times*, or the *Washington Post*; get stock market quotations; check the price of gold; send electronic mail to anyone who subscribes to the same data bank service; send Mailgrams to anyone; get medical information; or run one of the hundreds of programs always "on line" at the monster computer.

Data bank sharing offers an amazing array of services, all of which are accessible through the machine that everyone thought would only type letters.

One benefit of word processing in the office is that word processors are so quiet. The movements of fingers on a keyboard and the appearance of characters on a screen is very close to absolute silence. Some people find this quiet annoying after many years of "click-click-click," so some terminal manufacturers have added an electronic "click." After a weaning process, most people turn this feature off. If you buy a terminal that clicks, beeps or boops, make sure the noises can be turned off.

No denying that the printer is a noisy son-of-a-gun. It's about as loud as a Selectric being used full-tilt. However, the printer is usually not used as often as a Selectric. This is because many of the corrections that would normally require retyping have been discovered and corrected on the video screen. Further, since a fast letter-quality printer prints around 450 words per minute, the work is over relatively soon.

If noise is a major problem, the printer can be covered with a Plexiglas enclosure designed especially for silencing printers.

When asked by business people, "Should we buy now or should we wait? New and better computers are coming out every day." I reply, "Yes, there are, and buy it now."

Although personal computers will undoubtedly be less expensive in months and years to come, the money saved by increased efficiency and productivity will be far greater than whatever one might save by waiting.

Further, the office that buys a word processor now is clearly ahead of the game. Within a few years word processors and the work that they do will be standard. By the end of the decade an office without a word processor will be as passe as an office today without an electric typewriter.

As an example of this, take the personal letter. Presently, an individually typed, personalized letter means something. It gets noticed. Even if 500 other people got a letter that said the same thing, someone cared enough to order it personally typed. In five years everyone will know that preparing a personally typed letter on a word processor is only slightly more difficult than making a Xerox copy (less difficult if the Xerox machine is down the hall). Personally typed letters will lose their meaning. What will be the effect of a letter your secretary spends twenty minutes typing on her Selectric in 1986? It will hardly be noticed. By 1990 personally typed letters will be *expected*. Of course, by that time business letters will be considered almost quaint. The real movers and shakers in the business world will have taken to electronic mail years before.

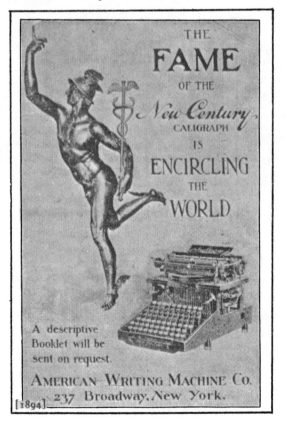

THE
FAME
OF THE
New Century,
CALIGRAPH
IS
ENCIRCLING
THE
WORLD

A descriptive Booklet will be sent on request.

AMERICAN WRITING MACHINE Co.
237 Broadway, New York.
[1894]

"Well, what do you think, Leo: Should we get a word processor?"

Chapter Six

Word Processing
and the Student

Within the next few years, personal computers will become the greatest Preppy status symbol since the alligator shirt. Lacoste, in fact, is planning on marketing a personal computer available in twelve designer colors with a little alligator in the corner of the video screen.

Personal computers like double-knit polo shirts are not for Preppies alone. We can all join in.

This chapter will examine what a personal computer, programmed for word processing, can do for students, be they high school, college, graduate students or "students of Life." The chapter will not deal so much with the educational possibilities of personal computers, although some of them will be mentioned later. The question answered in this chapter is, "What would happen if I sold my Smith-Corona portable typewriter to my little brother and got my parents to buy me a word processing computer?"

You may have noticed that this chapter is sandwiched neatly between a chapter on word processing in the office and word processing for the professional writer. This is no accident. As a student you are expected to record, organize and regurgitate material with the efficiency and accuracy of an executive secretary while maintaining a vast creative output and a literary style that ranges from the clarity of journalism to the imaginativeness of poetry. While this goal of student life, like absolute zero, can never quite be obtained, a word processor can offer certain tools that might prove valuable in the quest.

Reports. The bane of academic life. And a report by any other name — essay, thesis, term paper, biography, rhapsody, investigation — is still a report: take the information in, mix gently, put the information out. Original thought is generally not welcome, and creativity is limited to rearranging the professor's thoughts and comparing them favorably with the greatest minds of all time. On the whole it's dull work, but welcome to life.

There are "good study habits" that have been passed down through the eons of academia. A student with GSH on his or her way to a term paper would do something like this. (Let's see, shall I make this student a male or a female? I'll flip a coin: heads, male; tails, female. It was tails. This will be a female student with GSH.)

During class she takes copious notes. She does not go to the sock hop after class, she does not even pause for a cherry Coke. She goes directly to her room and types her notes while the lecture is still fresh in her mind. While she types, she elaborates upon the notes, remembering other information the professor gave in class and adding references to similar material from past classes. She notes the areas she does not understand and makes it a point to either ask the professor next day in class, ask one of her classmates for clarification, or research the unknown variable in the library. After researching it, of course, she will check with her mentor to make sure that Spinoza and the professor were saying the same thing. As term paper time rolls around she collates her notes, puts them in a comprehensible order, and writes her paper.

Like Sherlock Holmes, I doubt if this ideal student ever existed. I think she was created from all the "shoulds" that educators throughout time have laid upon themselves while they were in school but never bothered to follow. Using this as our ideal, however, let's see how a word processing computer might fit into this cycle of GSH.

The student would go home after class and type her notes. These would be her version, in her style, of what the professor had said. These would be stored on disks, and a copy could be printed daily or weekly for review. If there was a question, she could ask the professor in class, ask a classmate, or research it. Or she could write the professor a letter. Selecting passages from her notes, and disks from past classes, she could put together in just a few minutes a thoughtful, courteous, detailed, perfectly spelled and typed letter from a student who obviously must be very special. The answer to this letter is not nearly as important as the impression it would make. (Don't do this more than three times a semester. You don't want to cross the fine line between intellectual curiosity and stupidity.)

At term paper time her report is essentially written. All she does is pull from her disks the paragraphs she likes best, ties them together with a transitional sentence or two and prints a letter-perfect paper. While her fellow students are struggling to find (A) a topic and (B) a typist, our student with GSH (and a word processor) is at the student union enjoying a cherry Coke and looking forward to an uncrowded sock hop.

Whatever writing you do will go more smoothly and faster on a word processor. The key to good writing is editing. Most people include too much. With a word processor you can remove the verbiage without the penalty of retyping. You can be much freer in your expression, knowing that you can tighten as much as you like later.

After a paper is written, printed, graded and returned, it is easy to pull the paper up on the screen, make the changes and corrections recommended by the teacher, print a revised copy, and resubmit it. This takes little time and, although it may not alter your grade for that paper, it will give you brownie points galore. When was the last time you heard of anyone *voluntarily* rewriting a paper?

Some people cheat, of course, and buy other people's term papers. It is, in fact, a huge business with some mail-order companies offering tens of thousands of term papers on every imaginable subject.

I have mixed feelings about the practice of buying term papers. On one hand, it is cheating, it is dishonest, and if you're not willing to do the work, why on earth are you in school anyway? On the other hand, if you're a drama major and are forced to write a paper on medieval French tapestry to fulfill some obscure university requirement, then I can see that spending several days researching such a paper would be counterproductive and may interfere with one's education, which might be better served by memorizing lines or painting scenery. Reading a pre-written essay on medieval French tapestry just before adding one's name to it might teach a drama major all he or she would ever need to know on that particular subject.

I suppose that, like so much else in life, prewritten essays can be used either for or against an individual. If they're used to create time for learning about the subject near and dear to one's heart, they may be beneficial. If they're used to avoid learning necessary lessons of discipline and to support the illusion that an education or any other internal experience can be purchased like a new car, then prewritten papers might prove harmful.

Now, if you are in the former category and are buying essays on medieval French tapestry to create more time for your dramatic studies, or buying essays on drama to create more time for your medieval French tapestry, then the word processor can help. Let's say you buy the essay and transfer it to the computer. You can then go through and rewrite it to suit your personal style. (See the chapter **Poetry From A Computer** and the way in which *Little Miss Muffet* was "updated.") This is easy and the results far more convincing than simply adding one's name to someone else's style.

Of course, it would be easier if you didn't have to type the whole essay into the computer in the first place. Some enterprising entrepreneur will soon offer prewritten papers on disks ready to run on almost any word processor, and this person will no doubt make a fortune. Am I encouraging this? No. But if someone becomes a millionaire from reading this paragraph, I want a share.

At times in school — not often, but at times — you will be asked to create some original prose or poetry. A major mistake nonwriters (and a great many writers, myself at the head of the line) make is to think that before our sentences ever meet paper they must be perfect. This is the cause of writer's block. It's not that the writer cannot think of anything to write, it's that he or she cannot think of anything *perfect* to write.

There is a theory that the first step in creative writing is to write down anything and everything that comes to mind. The next step is to edit, emphasizing that which is good and removing that which is not.

Once one becomes accustomed to the ease with which changes are made on word processors, it becomes easier to write more and more, take more risks, go for ideas first and perfection later. It is not a magic wand, and we do not overnight become James Joyce, or even Jack Kerouac, but, given time, a freeing of expression does take place.

Teachers for some time now have ingrained in us the concept that an inability to spell automatically equals an inability to think. The only person who couldn't spell but who *could* think, in the opinion of most English professors, was Chaucer. You can write a paper that may contain some of the best prose and finest new ideas of the Western world and, if you misspell 10% of the words, you'll be hard pressed to find an educator who will take any of it seriously. Poor spelling equals dumb.

This, of course, is not true. At least I hope it's not true. Spelling requires an ability to inhale and exhale information verbatim, rather like being able to remember that 6 times 8 equals um, uh, let's see, 5 times 8 is 40, plus 8, okay... rather like being able to remember that 6 times 8 equals 48. I'm sure we all know people who can rattle off the times tables, can spell any word and are, in fact, creative wastelands.

Although it's not true that poor spelling equals dumb, it's still a belief, and a widely held belief that is not true is known by a difficult word to spell, prejudice. So, either you wage a one-person campaign against this prejudice (and if you do, you can count on me for a small but heartfelt contribution) or you can conform. Alas, it seems that one of the most painful portions of the educational process is deciding which bits of cultural nonsense we're going to take a stand against and which we're going to conform to. If we take a stand against *all* of them we are totally ignored, or locked up, or both. It seems as though we must pick our top six or seven dozen causes, flail against them with great vigor, and let the rest go.

If spelling is one you've decided to let go, the computer can help. As mentioned in the chapter on **The Curse of Noah Webster**, a word processor with a spell check program can locate most misspellings and can help you find the socially acceptable spellings. For the student who has spent hours over a dictionary looking up almost every word, knowing that the teacher was a Noah Webster groupie, and *still* missing a word or two, this feature of word processing will drift into that student's life like manna from heaven.

An interesting thing has been happening since I've been using my word processor to check for spelling errors. Rather than becoming a crutch, the word processor has actually improved my spelling. This surprised me. I thought I was a hopeless case. I had tried everything — flash cards, *Reader's Digest's* "Toward a More Powerful Vocabulary," Misspellers Anonymous ("I am helpless against my inability to spell..."), everything. I had given up.

I was great at finding synonyms. Whenever the word I wanted to use was too difficult to spell I would find one that was easier. I would never, for example, tackle the word "synonyms." I would write "similar words" or "words that mean the same thing," "similar" being a tough one too. I also found that after looking up all the words I *thought* were misspelled, they were usually spelled correctly in the first place. This was very frustrating.

I found that after getting a list of misspelled words, and misspelled words only, from the computer, and then finding the correct spellings for these words, somehow the acceptable-to-Mr.-Webster version began to sink in. I would notice patterns. I would put too many "Ms" in "coming" and too few "Ns" in "beginning." I tended to drop the final "E" before adding "ly." Things like that.

Now I make a game of it. I have the computer mark all the words that are misspelled and I have one chance to see if I can come up with the correct spelling. I'm getting about 50% of them. ("Space Invaders" was never this exciting.)

The fact is that I, like most "poor spellers," *do* know how to spell most words. It's the ones we *don't* know how to spell that give us trouble, and the pattern of these words tends to be as individual as our fingerprints. Knowing which words are our individual trouble makers and then discovering the correct spelling for them is the best way I have found for spelling improvement.

A personal computer is more than a word processor, just as a cassette recorder can be used to play more than Biology lectures. Many other programs available for personal computers can be of value to students.

Personal finance, for example, can do everything from helping you create a budget to balancing your checkbook. A math program can turn your computer into an electronic slide rule and beyond. You can chart your biorhythms or cast your horoscope. The programs offered for personal computers are endless. Like phonograph records, some are of value, many are not.

Then there are the programs that will actually teach you something. Computers are the perfect teacher. They will take you as far as you want as fast as you want, while providing limitless judgment-free tutorials in subjects you may find particularly difficult. If a student were a whiz at English Lit but found math incomprehensible the computer would take him quickly on beyond Beowulf while patiently letting him know that 2 + 2 does not equal 5.

There are programs that will teach you a skill necessary to operate a word processor: typing. If you don't know how to type now, don't worry. It's not hard to learn and you'll be glad that you did.

As described in the last chapter a personal computer can be connected via telephone to very large computers with massive data banks. These not only provide access to what is going on in the world (UPI newswire, the electronic editions of various newspapers, etc.) but also permit detailed research into what has already taken place. If you were researching our old friend, medieval French tapestry, you could enter the word "TAPESTRY" in the computer and receive a great deal of information on tapestry. Any time the word was used in the *New York Times*, for example, the article using that word would be instantly available. If the information was useful you could store it on disks for later reference; if not, you go on to the next article.

While we're discussing "other uses" for a computer, may I suggest that you *not* buy a computer that plays the flashy, full-color, complete with sound effects games? These are addictive, it seems, and your room will become an arcade and not a temple of Higher Learning. Enough said. A word to the wise is sufficient. Missile Command and Snafu are my favorites.

Beyond all this, a personal computer will give a student a skill that is valuable today, invaluable in five years and necessary in ten: computer literacy. Computer literacy is simply knowing how to use a computer, how to access it, how to add information to it and take information from it. Most importantly, computer literacy is being comfortable with computers, treating them as tools and not gods; with respect for, and not in fear of, their power. The best way to learn is by doing, and the best way to do is by owning a computer of one's own. It's the greatest investment parents can make in their child's future.

STUDENTS: Remove this page and send the rest of this chapter to your parents, along with your report card and a list of upcoming holidays, including your birthday. You can take out the part about cheating on term papers, but they'll like the idea of not playing games.

It might help if you misspell a few words in the note and make the handwriting occasionally illegible.

Good luck!

Chapter Seven

Word Processing

for

Writers

The past thirty years have not been kind to those of us homesteading on the printed page. Flashy technological innovations — from television to long-playing-stereophonic-high fidelity-phonograph-records to transistor radios to six-track-Dolby-stereo-seventy-millimeter-Technicolor-Panavision-SensurroundSound-Plus-motion pictures — have led people farther and farther from the written word.

One hundred years ago the Home Entertainment Center consisted of a bookcase. For a handful of highly sophisticated individuals Home Entertainment meant listening to the gramophone by gaslight; but for most, reading a book by candlelight was the way to spend an evening. The major outside-the-home entertainments of the early 1880s were concerts, musicales, plays and expositions. Parties were popular, from the rural quilting bees and barn raisings to the urban balls and socials. People also seemed to *enjoy* each other, and published recollections of the day refer to something known as **conversation** as being "stimulating" and "amusing."

These few distractions aside, it was a great time for the written word.

Fifty years ago, an occasional player piano or phonograph was beginning to take some readers from reading, but the real competition books faced was from radio which was about to enter its Golden Age. Away from home in the early 1930s, the talkies learned how to sing and Busby Berkeley taught them how to dance. Tickets were cheap and vaudeville was dying, so "a night out" almost always included a movie and maybe a little dancing. References to that form of entertainment known as "conversation" were growing fewer and farther between.

Reading was still popular, however. Thanks to mass education the literacy rate had risen; thanks to mass production the retail cost of a book had dropped (hardcover bestsellers could be had for about "a dollar the copy"); and thanks to mass greed the number of publishers publishing had increased dramatically. Some say this was the Golden Age of the American Novel.

Today the Home Entertainment center features a six-foot color television which can show video tapes, video disks, twenty-six channels of cable, seventy-nine channels of satellite programming, and more than one hundred video games; a stereo that plays digitally-recorded-half-speed-mastered records, Dolby encoded metal cassette tapes, and two-dozen stations of FM Multiplex radio; all this connected to a remote master   control unit that allows you to manipulate everything from the comfort of your redwood hot tub.

Clearly, there is no reason to leave the house, much less read anything more significant than the operator's manual for the latest technological goodie. If one ever does leave the house to purchase a new video tape or buy chlorine for the hot tub, one need not leave this Audio-Visual Disneyland behind. Car stereos, portable television/radios and light-weight-full-fidelity-tape-players-with-earphones make reading even a *National Enquirer* while waiting in line at the supermarket unnecessary.

Yes, technology has robbed us of a generation of readers. Not only are there far more dazzling alternatives to cracking a book but, thanks to these modern marvels, the literacy rate in this country is on the decline.

What has technology given writers in return? Well, let's see. In 1780 steel point pens were invented, light years ahead of the quill, which had plagued writers and various feathered birds since 600 B.C. In 1884 came the fountain pen: no more dipping. Ball points rolled along (sorry) around 1944. Remember the PaperMate PiggyBack pen that Art Linkletter claimed "writes through butter?" A great boon to writers moonlighting as short order cooks. Today we have such marvels as the felt tip pen (even with nylon points they're still called "felt tip pens") and the Erasable Ballpoint.

Typewriters were introduced a bit before fountain pens in 1874. They were produced by a manufacturer of fire arms, E. Remington and Sons. (The Remington Typewriter and the Remington Rifle both share the same birthplace, one of those quirks of history, like Pulitzer, who made his fortune from yellow journalism, presenting certificates for excellence in writing; or Nobel, the inventor of dynamite, awarding Peace Prizes.) Electric typewriters came along in 1920, the IBM Ball made its debut in 1961, and the correcting Selectric in the mid-1970s.

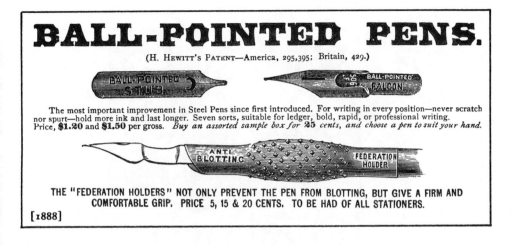

"Rejoice! Rejoice!
The steel tip pen
has been invented!"

Works Swiftly

Wears
—
Slowly

Remington
Standard Typewriter

Looking back on this 2,500 year history of writing technology one would have to answer our original question, "What has technology given writers in return?" with a conditional "Not much." Not much, that is, until today.

Word processing computers are sufficiently wonderful to forgive Science for its two-and-a-half millennia of foot dragging. Granted, word processors were not invented for creative writers. They were invented, like the steel point and the fountain pen and the typewriter and all the rest, for businesses. So even if Science did not set out intentionally to rectify centuries of injustice to writers, the end result is so glorious that we can grant them a general amnesty just the same.

It all started with journalists. Journalists used to be called "newspapermen," then women's lib came along and changed it to "newspaperpersons." This sounded silly, so the Federated Newswriter's Union (FNU) hired Image Consultants Inc., a public relations firm, to come up with a new handle for those working in the newspaper industry. Image Consultants (IC) gained notoriety when they changed the term "janitor" to "Sanitation Engineer."

IC, after months of deliberation and research, settled upon the term "Journalist." It was dignified, historical, nonsexist, and more than 70% of the newspaperpersons polled knew how to spell it. It was a natural. The FNU approved, changed their name to the FJU, and embarked on a multi-hundred-dollar campaign to etch the word "journalist" upon the soul of every literate human. IC has since been hired by the graduate students of Montana State University where they are working on an alternative name for the major "Meat Science."

Journalists work for big newspapers that have big computers to do payroll and accounts receivable and financial stuff like that. About fifteen years ago someone said, "If this computer can help the accounting department write checks, maybe it can help the reporters write stories." It could and it did.

Computer terminals replaced typewriters in newsrooms across the land. Clark Kent transformed into, not Superman, but Captain Video. Journalists kept quiet about it, though. The idea that the paper was being written by a computer would not have gone over very well fifteen years ago, and the male of the journalist species preferred to maintain his former image: cigar in mouth, Scotch in hand, pounding out a story on his trusty Remington Upright.

As some journalists moved on to the greener pastures of academic professorship, they discovered that they missed the ease and convenience of computer writing. They also discovered that Big Universities, like Big Newspapers, had Big Computers. Soon dissertations, theses, letters to mothers, and occasional term papers were rolling off University computers.

As the Seventies came limping in, the disagreement in Vietnam winding down, Richard Milhous Nixon as our President, the sum total of computer-assisted creative writing in this country were stories about lost dogs and lost innocence on one hand, and, on the other, scholarly tomes on the effect of Sixteenth Century chivalry upon the mercantile industry of the late 1700s. Plus a few letters to mothers. And so it remained for the next several years.

Then, something happened in the mid-1970s to change all that: the personal computer. No doubt science fiction writers had them first; it's their job to be on the cutting edge of such things. Then graduates of universities who missed the computer more than spring break. Then former-journalists-turned-novelists who wanted to look again at a TV screen with words on it. Then the friends of these pioneers, then the Sons of the Pioneers, then Roy Rogers, Dale Evans and, well, just about every writer or would-be writer around. It was an epidemic, far more contagious and far more real than the Swine Flu.

If you're a writer and you've read this far, I'm sure you're well aware of the ways in which word processors can enhance and assist the writing process. To review a few of them:

1. Change is effortless. Adding to, taking from, and moving around of text is simple. The changes are displayed at once, neatly "typed" on the video screen, with no cross-outs, " ^ " marks or scribbles in the margin.

2. Retyping is unnecessary. Even after a manuscript is printed and an error or area of improvement is discovered, all one needs to do is bring up the original on the video screen, make the change, and print a new page. Simple changes take but a few minutes, and most of that time is spent waiting for the printer. Only the changes need be typed. No more agonizing over whether the replacement of one word is worth retyping a whole page. Manuscripts are neat and free from penciled-in changes.

3. Spelling is perfect. Spelling and typing errors are detected by the computer. My mother feels that she must clean house before she can call a cleaning lady. Many writers feel that way about proofreaders: They're there to verify the perfection of the piece, not to correct it. Spell-check programs will let you know that every word in your text is a genuine, properly spelled word. Whether those words are used correctly or creatively is another story. There is, however a program that will help with grammar and punctuation. (See *Chapter Thirteen* **A Brand Name Buying Guide.**

4. Word processors are quiet. I remember advertisements for Exercycle from the 1960s. There was a photograph of a man exercycling away next to a bed, and on the bed was a woman smilingly asleep. (Back in the 1960s one automatically assumed this was his wife.) Under the photograph was written: "Exercycle: So Quiet He Can Exercise While She Sleeps."

I think the same approach can be used to sell word processors. At the word processor sits a Barbara Cartland type, smilingly writing away, and in bed lies a 19-year-old hunk, smilingly asleep. The caption would read, "Word Processors: So Quiet She Can Write While He Sleeps."

I think, too, it would be interesting to record a version of LeRoy Anderson's "The Typewriter Song" entitled "The Word Processor Song." The portions of the song devoted to typewriter clicking would be silent.

Until it comes time to print something, word processors are blessedly quiet. If neighbors, roommates, lovers, or spouses have narrowed your hours of typewriter writing, word processing will provide you with a lengthened creative day. In a pinch you can even write in the dark. Just to see if that last sentence were true, I turned off the lights and am writing this in total darkness, the keyboard being illuminated only by the light of the video screen. If you can watch TV with earphones and not disturb the slumber of another, then you could write with a word processor as well.

5. You are not chained to a typewriter table. The detachable keyboard, available on many personal computers, is wonderful. As I write this the keyboard is on my lap. With an extension, I could lie down and write, take the keyboard out on the patio (if I had à patio), or even use it in the bathroom. The long hours of sitting in the one position necessary to operate a stationary typewriter with the cramps and tensions caused by that position are no more.

6. No more carriage returns. Most word processing programs automatically place the next word on the next line when the right hand margin is reached. In this way the words can flow and you need only hit the carriage-return button when you want to start a new paragraph. No more little bells telling you that in eight more keystrokes your typewriter will stop dead.

7. Correspondence is easy. How often have you wanted to write essentially the same thing to five friends? In circulating this information you might get off a letter or two before boredom ("I have to type that *again*") or guilt ("I should be writing my book and not these letters") encourage you to abandon the project. With a word processor all you have to write is one letter and print out five copies, changing only the recipient's name each time. *I* know this is a form letter, and *you* know this is a form letter, but *they* won't know it's a form letter, unless, of course, they too have a word processor, in which case they are probably sending you form letters already.

There are other form letters you may want to send out. In selling your works, it will no doubt be necessary to circulate a series of letters each saying the same thing, to a variety of people: editors, publishers, agents, mothers. These must be individually typed and personalized to the recipient; a Xerox copy simply wouldn't do. In the same way that personalized form letters can help a businessman make a sale, personalized form letters can help you make a sale, too.

Some writers maintain their correspondence but feel that they should be keeping a journal as well; others keep a journal but fall behind in their correspondence. With a word processor you can do both. If you enjoy correspondence, you can write about your life in letters to your friends, then choose the best paragraphs and copy them into your electronic journal. If journal-keeping is your preference, write your journal on the word processor then send excerpts in the form of letters to your friends. In this way, both literary traditions are maintained.

8. Research is easier. Using the data banks, discussed in the previous two chapters, researching a project that might have required many trips to the library and much correspondence can often take place in the comfort of your own computer terminal.

9. Other programs are available. Writers seldom have one-track minds; their interests are broad, passionate, and varied. The many programs that can be run on personal computers when they're not being used for word processing might prove invaluable in satisfying a writer's greatest passion: curiosity. (All right, a writer's second greatest passion.)

10. They're fun. Computers are great, expensive, fascinating toys. As a writer you can justify the purchase of such a toy to just about anyone, including the taxman. (In most cases. See your accountant or the Tax People at H & R Block for full details. Located at larger Sears, J.C. Penney and Montgomery Wards stores coast to coast. Offer void where prohibited by law. Subject to cancellation without notice.)

If you're a writer, and if you're anything like me, you turned to this chapter first. I encourage you to read that which came before it, and that which follows, to get a true picture of how word processors might serve you in the creation of your work.

I have made my living as a writer for fifteen years, and nothing — not a correcting Selectric, not a personal secretary, not even a #1 *New York Times* best seller — has thrilled or inspired me to write more than my word processor. All these years, writing has been a chore, a job, work. It's still a job, it's still work but, thanks to the word processor, every so often, more and more often, writing is a joy.

(Any advertising agency that would like to use that last paragraph as copy for the "Word Processors: So Quiet She Can Write While He Sleeps" ad, please be in touch. I work cheap and am not afraid of selling out if the price is right, which it almost always is.)

Here we have a typical writer's workspace using a word processor. Can you find: (A) The keyboard, (B) The Video Screen, (C) Quart of Haagen-Dazs Ice Cream (Maple Walnut), (D) The computer (look for the black square indicating the disk drives), (E) Quart of Haagen-Dazs Ice Cream (Vanilla Chocolate Chip), (F) File to hold floppy disks, (G) Four months of neglected correspondence.

And here is another view of that same creative corner. Can you find: (A) The keyboard, (B) Portrait of Gertrude Stein by Picasso, (C) Computer, (D) Portrait of Picasso by Picasso, (E) Printer, (F) Plastic knife holding light switch in place, (G) Comfortable chair.

"FINE LARGE CUCUMBERS!"

Chapter Eight

Word Processing
and the Self-Employed

A great many people work for themselves. They are the self-employed. They own and operate their own small businesses, everything from dry cleaners to farms to mail order companies. They are The Professionals: doctors, lawyers and psychologists. They are the ones who put the words "free lance" in front of whatever it is they do. They are sales people working on commissions. They are the creative people, from artists to dancers to inventors.

As diverse as their occupations might be, the self-employed all have one thing in common: The money they make is linked to their own initiative and is directly affected by what they do, how often they do it, and how effectively they get it done. For a great many of the self-employed, "getting it done" can significantly be aided and abetted by a word processing computer.

Let's look at a variety of occupations, from psychologist to plumber to bookstore owner, and see how a word processing computer might prove useful. If you are among the ranks of the self employed, we probably won't touch directly upon your particular business. You may find, however, that some of the ideas presented in this chapter will adapt to your working situation.

" KNIVES TO GRIND !"

A physician, psychologist, psychiatrist, chiropractor, counselor or health professional of any kind could use a word processor to keep in closer contact with his or her clients. With medical financial software, the computer could also handle billing, insurance forms and a variety of client records. Let's see how one psychologist, Amble, does it.

Amble is a caring man. He has deep concern for each of his clients. He is also a voracious reader and every so often comes across an idea or a quotation or a thought that he would like to share with his friends and clients alike.

Amble has more than a hundred clients and a like number of friends. He's not about to begin a newsletter, and the concept of a mimeographed intimate letter is out of the question. For a solution, he turns to his trusty word processor.

Using a prepared mailing list, Amble can turn out 200 personalized letters, with envelopes, in an afternoon. He signs each letter personally and can, if he likes, add a hand written postscript.

To the recipient, the letter looks hand typed, and indeed it is: Amble personally typed the letter into the computer; fed the sheets into the printer; stuffed, licked and stamped the envelopes himself. He feels more a part of each letter than if he had paid a secretary to type each letter individually.

Some may find it cold and uncaring to do a computer mailing to friends and clients. This concept no doubt comes from the hundreds of "personalized" computer letters we've received from cold and uncaring companies who wanted only one thing from us: our money.

In fact, Amble genuinely wants to share the information in the letter with each person on his list. If he had the time (and ability) he would type or write each letter by hand. But, like most of us, he does not have the time, and his word processor is the tool he uses to turn a loving thought into a loving deed.

Like every other health professional he's ever met, Amble has a book or two in him. Rather than tackle a project as large as a book head on, Amble finds it easier to take it one chapter at a time. These chapters are written as articles for local newspapers and national magazines. This allows him to receive what he would term "positive strokes," for, although he would hesitate to admit it, Amble likes to see his name in print. He also likes seeing his name printed on checks. He enjoys reading the letters generated by his articles, and answers them, naturally, on his word processor.

Soon, with a dozen articles behind him, he begins the task of compiling a book, an editorial feat made infinitely easier by his word processing computer.

Amble also uses the word processor to remind him of client birthdays and other events he wishes to celebrate. At least one birthday cake per week is consumed in Amble's office. Amble is particularly fond of birthday cake.

The computer is used for client billing, for insurance forms and for managing Amble's personal finances, an area of his life for which he has a disregard bordering on contempt. With his accountant, a tax whiz, he chose a computer program that would record all the information necessary for the accountant to prepare the necessary returns. Amble dutifully enters this information into the computer. It is a test of discipline. He looks upon it as a Zen exercise. He finds that his computer is a far more agreeable partner in the task of fiscal management than were the books with rows of numbers provided him by his accountant in the past.

Amble has given his personal computer a name, refers to it as his "friend and colleague," and every so often considers making it a full partner in his practice.

" FINE ORANGES ! "

"MILK BELOW, MAIDS!"

Let's take a look at another self-employed individual, Joe Ann the plumber. Joe Ann purchased her word processor to write a book about her adventures as the first woman plumber of Santa Monica, California. The style of the book, she decided, would be somewhere between Cervantes and Erma Bombeck. Joe Ann soon discovered, much to her dismay, that she could not write. She knew that plumbing required skill, training, and no small degree of inborn talent, but it never occurred to her that writing might require the same qualities.

After several weeks of struggle she put the word processor unceremoniously in the back of her truck and took it to the office. She planned to leave it in a deserted corner and write it off as a tax loss later that year.

Her secretary, Michael, adopted the machine at once. Michael was in charge of bookkeeping and correspondence. "He's the one who types; I take care of the pipes," Joe Ann would explain.

Michael immediately transferred to the computer the form letters he typed several times each day: estimate letters, follow-up letters, contractual letters, thank you letters, request for payment letters. These routine letters which usually consumed several hours each day, were soon taken care of in less than an hour.

New form letters were created. How was the work we did six months ago and is there anything we can help you with today? How was the work we did a year ago and is there anything we can help you with today?

They began sending out personalized letters on specific subjects to everyone on their mailing list. Do you have a drain that Drano won't help? It's Check Your Water Heater Month! How's your septic tank?

Joe Ann and Michael, buoyed by the success of these mailings, began buying mailing lists of local home owners and sending them personalized letters introducing them to Joe Ann, Santa Monica's First Woman Plumber. The response was heartening.

Meanwhile, Michael was investigating bookkeeping programs and finally purchased one. Slowly he went from paper to electronic billing. As Michael wisely noted, learning how to generate form letters on the computer took a few days; learning how to keep books on the computer would take awhile longer.

Within a year's time business increased to the point where Joe Ann could hire two "fellow" woman plumbers. She didn't discriminate — they were simply the best-qualified persons for the job. And, although his output has increased, Michael is able to still take care of the typing while Joe Ann and Company take care of the piping.

Michael, in fact, finds that he has enough free time to work on a book. Using the word processor, he's writing about his adventures working for Santa Monica's First Computerized Woman Plumber.

In the small town of Prospect, Ohio, Mrs. Wicks owns and operates Wicks Book Store. Although her inventory is one-fourth that of the Big City book store just down the street, Mrs. Wicks sells more books than they do. This is because Mrs. Wicks cares about every book and every person that goes through her store.

Mrs. Wicks, a retired school teacher, loves books. She loves people, too, especially people who love books. Her gift is remembering what subjects her customers like and notifying them of new titles as they become available.

As more and more people let Mrs. Wicks know their areas of interest, she began cross-referencing these in a card file. Eventually she got a computer. "It was either hire someone or buy a computer." Mrs. Wicks explains. "I decided I'd get on better with a computer."

Mrs. Wicks carefully reads all publisher's catalogs and book announcements in *Publisher's Weekly* and the *Ingram Trade Advance*. Popular books she orders, and when they arrive she sends out personalized letters announcing their arrival to interested readers:

> Borta O'Hara's latest novel, "Love's Mad, Tender, Passionate Embrace of Torrid Desire" is now in stock. This is Ms. O'Hara's first book since "Passion's Potent Potion," which came out last week, and is said to be her best novel since last month's "Rapture Erupts." Due in next Friday: "Uncle Tom's Passion."

For books with limited appeal, Mrs. Wicks sends a letter informing the customers that the book is in print and can be special ordered:

> The latest book on health food, "Don't Eat Yogurt---They Put Bacteria in It!" is now in print and I can order it for you. Chapters include "MSG and the CIA," "Go Yeast Young Man" and "How to Make Solar Granola."

Mrs. Wicks has her word processor print out reply cards, which are included with each letter. These have the titles of the books suggested, the customer's name and address, and possible methods of payment.

The customer, after reading the letter, need only check the appropriate boxes and place the return reply card in the return reply envelope, thoughtfully — and cleverly — enclosed by Mrs. Wicks.

This is the return mail card of Mr. John Doe, a man who, according to Mrs. Wicks's computer, likes books on cooking, Watergate, sex education, and making money:

Dear Mrs. Wicks, Please send me:

_____ copies "Joy of Cooking Sex" ($9.95)

_____ copies "I Know How to Be Really Rich and You Don't" ($25.00)

_____ copies "The Last Whole Nixon Catalog" ($1.75)

_____ Please bill to my account.

_____ Check enclosed

Charge to my

_____ Visa _____ MasterCard

Number: _____

Expiration Date:_____

_____Mail books to me.

_____Hold books at the store.

_____Call me when they arrive.

Thank you very much.

John Doe

123 Main Street

Anytown, Ohio

12345

Although her inventory is several hundred thousand dollars less than the Big City bookstore down the street, is it any wonder that Mrs. Wicks and her $6,000 word processing computer sometimes get the feeling that they are the only bookstore in town?

"FRESH OYSTERS! PENNY A LOT!"

I could sit here imagining word processing applications for imaginary businesses all night — come to think of it, I already have. If you are self-employed, I invite you to join in this brainstorming with me: If you had a machine that did all the things described in this book sitting in front of you right now, how might it benefit your business? How might it help you serve those for whom you do your work? How might it make you, or someone who works for you, more productive? How might it help you generate more business? How might it help you organize the business you already have?

Word processing computers are not magic wands. They will not, in and of themselves, save a dying company. They will not turn a poor business person into an entrepreneur.

A word processor is a powerful tool that, when used with intelligence and creativity, will lead the self-employed individual several steps closer to the goals of success, abundance, and personal freedom.

"PINS, NEW PINS!"

Chapter Nine

Poetry from a Computer?

**Being a Chapter on the Only Taboo
in America That Has Not Been the
Subject of a Movie of the Week**

We all know about poets and we all know about computers. Poets and computers populate distant extremes on the Continuum of Existence. Poets are ephemeral, fey, ultrasensitive unicorns living on air and inspiration, usually consumed by consumption before the age of thirty. Computers are hard, exacting, unforgiving amalgamations of steel and silicon, designed by scientists to serve Big Business and Big Government in exacting from us what little money and freedom we may have left.

Yes, we all know about poets and we all know about computers. The idea of a poet using a computer to create poetry is about as foreign to most people as the Taj Mahal. Yet it's happening every day, at great Universities, in Computer-Land stores and in stereotypical poet's hovels all over the country: Poets are Poeting and they're doing it on computers.

I have actually written poetry on a computer. There, I said it and I'm glad. I didn't set out to write a self-confessional chapter. I thought I could objectively review this controversial subject from a detached point of view, but in the end I could not stoop to journalism. I had to tell you the truth about myself, and I'm willing to take the consequences.

I know, of course, that this means no Pulitzer Prize, at least during my lifetime. (It wasn't until 1953 that the Pulitzer Committee would even consider poetry written on a *typewriter*.) I know that the sale of my next book of verse will be limited to a few computer enthusiasts who also happen to like poetry (twelve, in all). I know that the poetry journals will invent cruel jibes and hurl them at me. They'll call me The Poet Laureate of Radio Shack, and snigger behind their quills.

But I'm strong. I can take it. I don't want to take it, but I can take it. And, quite frankly, I'd rather take it than return to the land of pen and ink, of constant retyping, of watching cherished, beloved poems go in one end of a Xerox machine and not come out the other. "Must like poetry," the machine operator would chuckle. No, I'll take it, and I'll be vindicated by the future, just as I am already vindicated by history.

The first poet to use a word processor was Milton. He was blinded in 1652 and used his daughter as an instrument to write some of his finest works, including *Paradise Lost*. The actual processing of the words went on in Milton's mind. His daughter was there to record his thoughts; to read them back; to make whatever changes, deletions, or additions Milton deemed appropriate; and to recopy the final poem letter perfect for later publication — all the things modern-day computerized word processors do so well.

No doubt Milton was not the first to write poetry using the word processing capabilities of another. I'm sure that

leisurely poets from antiquity on have dictated their opuses to waiting scribes with better handwriting than they. Poets don't tend to admit this, however. The idea of struggling alone and forlorn for the ever-evasive couplet is an image that poets like to maintain. Writers other than poets don't seem to have qualms concerning a little outside help. Socrates had a word processor. His name was Plato. Milton could not avoid giving credit where credit was due. He was, after all, blind, and the Braille typewriter was more than two hundred years in the future.

The first person to ever write a poem on a word processing computer is difficult to pinpoint. No doubt some scientist, back in the days when computers were larger than Orson Welles, wrote a line or two immortalizing the sweetness of his loved one. The computer, dutiful servant that it was, printed the whole thing on a Valentine's Day Card without so much as a giggle.

By the time the computer-cum-word-processor got into the newsroom, closet Superpoets posing as mild-mannered reporters wrote verse after verse on screens of video. Late at night, of course. Long after the mere mortals were at home and in bed. Naturally, there were poets aplenty when computers-turned-word-processors eased onto the campus. Universities are, after all, the first and the last refuge of poets; Universities and Salvation Army Missions. Professorial types, pretending to be working on yet another dissertation, were in actuality dashing off a few more stanzas of their epic *An Ode on "An Ode on a Grecian Urn."*

But all that's history. There is more poetry today being written on computers than graffiti on subways. (I once saw a young man colorfully expressing his considered opinion of a local law enforcement agency on a formerly blank wall. Ever curious of my fellow writers and their possible use of word processing in any form, I asked him if he had ever tried writing graffiti on a computer. "Yeah," he said. "I was working for this company in the mail room and one night I was there late and I went into the computer room and tried writing some graffiti on one of the computers." How wonderful! I could see the title of my new book before me: **Graffiti in the Computer Age!** I could see the fan mail pouring in. I could see my royalty checks. "How did it turn out?" I asked, my eyes wide with interest. "Not too good," he said. "My spray can ran out of paint before I could finish.")

Why are poets turning to computers in record number?

Personal computers, outfitted with a quality word processing program, allow a writer maximum freedom to rearrange, take from, add to, alter, correct — in a word, change — the material being written. Of all writers, poets do more rearranging, taking from, adding to, altering, correcting — in a word, changing — than anyone else. Hence, the benefits of word processing accrue quickly for poets.

To demonstrate, let's take the work of that beloved poet, Isadora Goose, known affectionately to all as "Mother." Let us suppose that the well-known journal of poetics *Humpty Dumpty* asked me to update a few of Mrs. Goose's better-known poems. I would do it very much as Isadora herself might, if she were alive today with a word processor at her peck and call. Let's take the classic, *Little Miss Muffet.*

Little Miss Muffet
Sat on her tuffet
Eating her curds and whey.
Along came a spider
And sat down beside her
And frightened Miss Muffet away.

Now I know that I would have to keep the basic structure of the piece, maintaining the natural rhythm and as many rhymes as possible. My job is to update, not to rewrite.

The first word that stands out is "tuffet." A tuffet is either a mound of grass or a stool. Mother's meaning is not certain here. She states that Miss Muffet *owned* the tuffet when she said "Sat on *her* tuffet." However, the word "Little" seems to imply that Miss Muffet might be too young to be a landowner, hence "tuffet" may refer to stool or seat. Nonetheless, spiders are more commonly found out-of-doors on grassy tuffets. It is a puzzlement and great books have been written on this very subject by men and women far more learned than I.

The point is that you don't hear the word "tuffet" used very much in either context anymore. Real estate salespersons do not extol the wonders of a garden "with flower-beds, beautiful shrubbery, and several very nice tuffets." And advertisements do not appear saying, "Dining Room Set, complete with breakfront, buffet, table, and six tuffets." No, "tuffet" will have to go.

But what to replace it with? I like the idea that Ma Goose meant tuffet to mean stool. Too many poems have been written outside, going on and on about the beauty of the out-of-doors. We need more poems about the beauty of the in-of-doors. The nearest two-syllable word that means stool, remembering that we must keep the Goose's meter, is "barstool." Everyone knows what a barstool is, even the readers of *Humpty Dumpty.*

With the press of a few buttons on my word processor, I find the first two lines have become...

Little Miss Muffet
Sat on her barstool...

The "Muffet" part must go. It no longer rhymes. The "Miss" will, of course, become "Ms." In that light, "Little" seems a bit condescending, too. This whole first line is in need of an overhaul.

What's a contemporary rhyme for "barstool?" Why, of course, "carpool." Wonderful. Teach the kids the importance of conservation right from grade one. "Miss Muffet" is now "Ms. Carpool." We've lost an alliteration, though: the two "M's" in "Miss Muffet." And what about "Little?" What adjective describes this truly contemporary Ms. Carpool and begins with an "M?" Why, of course, "Modern."

Modern Ms. Carpool
Sat on her barstool
Eating her curds and whey.

"Curds and whey" is the solid and liquid parts of whole milk when it curdles. It was very popular back when people sat around on tuffets. It has since lost its popularity. It is doubtful that our Modern Ms. Carpool would be sitting at a bar eating curdled milk. A banana daiquiri, maybe; curdled milk, no. We are, however, writing for a children's magazine, so we can't make this *too* contemporary. She'll have to be eating some healthy dairy product.

Further, whatever she's eating will have to rhyme with "whey" because we want to keep as many of the original rhymes as possible, and we already departed from that in the first two lines: "Muffet" does not rhyme with "Carpool" no matter how far we stretch it.

What rhymes with "whey" and is a healthy dairy product? Simple: Yoplait, the brand name for a kind of yogurt. "Yoplait yogurt," unfortunately, does not rhyme with "curds and whey." We must invoke our poetic license and switch "Yoplait" and "yogurt" around, easy to do on a word processor.

Modern Ms. Carpool
Sat on her barstool
Eating her yogurt Yoplait.

Along came a spider
And sat down beside her...

The stuff about the spider is okay. I mean, it's traditional. Besides, "spider" and "beside her" make a great
rhyme. Then we come to the last line:

And frightened Miss Muffet away.

The obvious thing to do is to change "Miss Muffet" to
"Ms. Carpool" and collect one's box of Crayolas. But, no: there
is something very wrong with this line. In the first place,
would "Modern" Ms. Carpool really be frightened away by a
spider? I doubt it. She might not appreciate his company as
much as, say, John Travolta's, but to be frightened away? We
could end the poem with, Said she, "Would you please go
away?" making Ms. Carpool the graduate of an assertiveness
training group, but this, too, skirts the real issue.

Yes, the disparity is a deeper one. It goes to the very
core of one of our primary cultural taboos: unjustified
prejudice against spiders. Justified prejudice I can understand. People are prejudiced against mosquitos. Who can
blame them? It's justified. But where is the justification for
the prejudice against spiders? Nowhere. A few black widows
kill a few Sierra Club members every year, but so what? Cars
kill 50,000 people each year and we *love* cars. No, the
prejudice against spiders is unjustified.

Beyond that, spiders actually do good. They eat mosquitos and flies and all those other creepy-crawly things that
we have justifiable prejudices against. It's time we changed,
and change must come through education, and education
begins at bedtime with nursery rhymes. Let's make the spider
an ordinary sort of guy!

So, here we have our scenario: Ms. Carpool is sitting at
a bar eating yogurt. A spider comes along, sits down next to
her and, keeping in mind that he's a regular, normal person,
what does he do? Why, he orders something to eat, just like
Ms. Carpool.

But what would a spider order? "I'll have a Yoplait
Mosquito Yogurt, please." No. Spiders don't eat yogurt.
People eat yogurt. No point in making this a Walt Disney
movie. Spiders eat bugs. But going into a bar and ordering a
plate of bugs is rather unappetizing, so how do we add a little

class to the situation, and being locked into a rhyme pattern, rhyme his order with "Yoplait?"

Let's make this a gourmet spider. This means he would have to order bugs prepared in some French-sounding way, such as saute or flambee. Eating "bugs" is a bit weird, so we'll modify that just a bit, too. We add this last line to our Mother Goose Computerized Update, and, voila!

> **Modern Ms. Carpool**
> **Sat on her barstool**
> **Eating her yogurt Yoplait.**
> **Along came a spider**
> **And sat down beside her**
> **And ordered an insect souffle.**

There were twenty-six words in the original poem. By changing only eleven of them, less than half, the entire poem was transformed into something quite different. Fifteen words remained the same. With a word processor there was no need to retype even one of them.

Poetry from a Computer?

The nonsense above is a parody of what goes on in the creative mind as it refines, hones, and coaxes the English language into poetry. Yet behind the fun is a portrait of the actual word processor at work — the human mind. For the poet, a word processing computer is a tool that remembers and displays the best of what has gone on before; that makes experimental alterations quickly, silently, and with a minimum of effort; that awaits patiently, alert and ever-ready for the next command, be it in five seconds or five days. A tool such as this might just free the mind of the poet, allowing true poetry to flow through.

The real news is not that word processing computers will do for poets everything typewriters do, only more and better and faster. The real news will come as poets apply the many joys and wonders of word processors to the creation of new and remarkable forms of human expression for the illumination of us all.

PART III

Selecting and Purchasing
a Word Processing Computer

Chapter Ten

The Drawbacks of
Word Processing Computers

In discussing the drawbacks of any situation in life (and what would life be without its drawbacks?) there seem to be two extremes.

The first is to ignore all possible danger, the basic what-I-don't-know-won't-hurt-me attitude exemplified by ostriches and those living near nuclear power plants. The problem with this approach is that potential difficulties, if dealt with knowingly and practically, can often be eliminated or reduced. To paraphrase Law Enforcement's favorite cliche, Ignorance of the drawback is no excuse.

At the other end of the spectrum are those who focus on the drawback, only on the drawback and nothing but the drawback. These people seldom leave the house. They watch Geraldo Rivera on television tell them how terrible it is "out there." But in staying at home there is still a great deal to be worried about: burglars, household accidents, air pollution, and radiation beaming at them from their color TVs.

Most of us fall somewhere between those two extremes. We see both sides of an issue in the cool, calm light of reason and make our choices accordingly. We hope. Is life a rose bush with thorns or a thorn bush with roses?

In presenting a chapter on the drawbacks of word processing computers I am sure that I will get reactions from both extremist camps. One will skip the chapter altogether, "I really don't want to know." The other will use it as evidence not to read further, "See, I told you these things were no good."

The rest of us will, hopefully, view the possible drawbacks and the potential drawbacks from a creative point of view, looking for solutions as we go.

Here, then, are the several possible drawbacks of word processing computers I have come upon.

1. They're expensive. Lanier calls their word processing system "No Problem." What about the problem of coming up with the money? No way around it — Several thousand dollars is a lot of dollars. Word processors do do a great deal, and there is a price to be paid.

On one hand, they cost a lot. On the other hand, they are a great value. An IBM Selectric costs around $1,000. A word processing computer costs five to ten times that amount. A word processor, however, will do far more than five to ten times the work of a Selectric. When word processors are used in a business or professional setting, depending on the application, they often pay for themselves in a short time.

The prices keep going down. I paid around $7,500 for mine. Three months later I could have purchased a word processor with the same capabilities and specifications for $6,000. However, in those three months I more than earned the $1,500 difference. To buy now or to wait? To buy at all? The information in the next chapter, **Is Word Processing for You?**, may help you decide.

2. Eyestrain, neck strain, and back strain. Some people are more susceptible to eyestrain when looking at a video screen than are others. If you have frequent headaches from watching regular television you might be one of these people. You could also be having a natural reaction to most television programming. You might want to rent a word processor for a week or so and see how you feel using it. Most people do not have this sensitivity.

Word processing generally does not involve staring constantly at a video screen. It involves looking at the screen, looking at the keyboard, looking at some notes, and, if you're like me, looking out the window, looking in the refrigerator, and looking for the perfect excuse to "finish it later."

Most eye, neck, and back strain is caused by improper lighting or improper placement of the keyboard and video screen. Improper lighting will cause glare on the video screen, a major cause of eye fatigue. Poor placement of the video screen and keyboard leads to poor posture and awkward positions, causing neck and back strain.

Filters are available that cover the video screen. These filters improve the contrast of the characters and reduce reflected glare. If eyestrain is a problem, one of these filters might help.

3. Radiation. All television screens give off some form of radiation. This is true of home television sets as well as computer video screens. Some people must stare into video screens at close range for long periods of time — military personnel watching radar, for example, or text editors who do nothing but edit other people's material all day.

There are isolated incidences of cataracts in those who

must look continuously into a video screen at point-blank range for long periods of time. These incidents are very small in proportion to the tens of thousands of people who stare into computer screens every day.

It is supposed that low-level radiation caused the cataracts. Radiation is something we cannot afford to treat lightly. "Acceptable" levels of low-level radiation are much lower than once thought. We cannot go about being fearful, either. To get rid of all low-level radiation would mean ridding ourselves of microwave ovens, all televisions, and the sun itself. The fact is, we do not know as much about the effects of low-level radiation upon human beings as we need to know.

We do know that all video screens, including regular home television sets, give off some radiation. We do know that color TVs usually give off more than do black & white. We do know that the farther away the screen is, the less the possible danger.

Based upon what we know, then, the safest way to use a word processing computer would be to use a black & white video screen and have the screen close enough to see the characters clearly but no closer — usually two to three feet. In most cases this will require a detachable keyboard. Also, if you have a large amount of detailed copy editing, it might be better to do that on a print-out rather than by peering into the video screen close-up for hours on end.

On the whole, there is no more to fear working at a word processor for a full day than there would be watching television for a comparable period of time.

4. Mistakes, when they happen, can be big ones. Short of a fire in a filing cabinet or shredding the wrong pile of confidential documents, it is almost impossible when working with sheets of paper to duplicate the magnitude of error possible on a computer.

The Random Access Memory of many computers can easily hold thirty pages of material and if the power fails before that information is transferred to disks it's back to square one. One little 5¼-inch disk can hold up to 600 pages of text. The following is a partial list of how those 600 pages can be permanently destroyed in less than a second:

Computer error. Every so often a computer will get hungry and eat a disk.

Operator error. Far more common than computer error. With a single mistaken command the information on a disk can be no more.

Paper clips. You know those paper clip dispensers that have a magnetic circle at the top to hold the paper clips until needed? While they're hanging on that magnet, the paper clips themselves are being magnetized. If one of these paper clips should fall on a disk, it would be the equivalent of dropping a red hot paper clip on a phonograph record.

Scissors. Many pairs of scissors, for a reason I have yet to discover, are magnetized. If these are set on top of a disk or a disk is set on top of them...

Ringing telephones. Apparently a ringing telephone produces a magnetic field that plays havoc with disks if the disks are under the phone. Why one would store their disks underneath a ringing phone is beyond me, but apparently some people do and they have had problems. (I have been unable to duplicate this problem myself.)

Food. Anything from spilled coffee to toasted marshmallows: If food lands on a disk it is not good for the disk.

Grease, oil, dirt. If you're eating buttered popcorn and changing a disk at the same time (I'm making myself hungry) and the oil gets on the inside of the disk, not good. Even the natural oil on the fingers, if smudged on the magnetic part of the disk, can cause the disk drive to mistrack.

Pens, ink, eraser gook. If you write on the label of a disk with a ball point pen it might ruin the disk. If you erase the label of a disk and the eraser stuff gets in the disk jacket, it can cause problems.

Et cetera. This category is for all the creative screw-ups people come up with: "My dog ate it," "Somebody stole it," and "I didn't know you were supposed to leave the cardboard *on* the disk." Et cetera.

The solutions to these potential dangers are: save material from RAM to disk frequently while editing; make back-up copies of disks often (discussed further in *Chapter Twelve*); keep magnetized objects away from the work area; and treat disks with the same care with which an audiophile would treat his or her record collection.

These are the four major drawbacks I've come across. From my point of view, they are not so much reasons to avoid word processing computers as they are areas in which due caution and respect for the machinery (and one's current budget) are in order.

"The dog ate it."

Chapter Eleven

Is Word Processing for You?

Is a word processing computer for you? That's simple: If you use a typewriter to write anything from a letter a day to a book a month, the answer is "Yes." "Is a word processing computer for you?" unfortunately is not the right question to ask. If you're reading this book, the answer is almost certain to be yes. A more accurate question, although not nearly as punchy, is: "Would my purchase of a word processing computer justify itself in terms of expense and the length of time it would take me to learn how to use it?" Now that's a relevant question; long, but relevant. Let's explore it.

A word processing computer complete with software and printer will set you back at least $2,500. It could go as high as $10,000. A decent, dependable processor that will turn out printed pages equal to the best electric typewriter will run around $5,000. In *Chapter Twelve*, **Selecting a Word Processing Computer,** we'll look at the reasons for this range of prices and what you can expect to get from various price categories.

Further, word processing computers take a while to master. Not much of a while, but a while. Someone who regularly uses a typewriter to do his or her work, from creative writing to correspondence, would be able to have a word processor mastered within a week. Addiction sets in within a month, and after two months going back to even the finest Selectric would seem almost intolerable.

For the secretary or writer who is used to a keyboard, the time it takes to adjust to a word processor is minimal. However, those who are not well versed in typing will need a bit more adjustment. How much adjustment depends upon how familiar one already is with a typewriter and how quickly one learns.

If you plan to use a word processor, some knowledge of typing is essential. Sorry, the computers that will print letter-perfect text from verbal dictation are still part of computing's future. Computers that will read back what you have typed into them are already here and work with a reasonable degree of accuracy. Perfect touch-typing is, thank heaven, not necessary. I get by with a modified hunt-and-peck system using two fingers (it doesn't really much matter which two) at a time.

I type about as fast as I can write longhand. Is a word processor valuable for someone who has far from mastered the keyboard? Absolutely. First of all, for those of us who are not good at typing, the very thought of *retyping* something is abhorrent. Typing is a tolerable way of transferring one's thoughts to paper, but to transfer one's thoughts from one piece of paper to another piece of paper is a waste of time and is drudgery beyond belief. Fortunately, word processors never ever require retyping — unless you make a mistake and erase a diskette or the computer makes a mistake and eats a diskette or some such other unthinkable event. On the whole retyping is out.

Second of all, mistakes, quite common to us inexperienced typists, are easy to correct on word processors. Typos are corrected with such speed and ease that there is almost no time to think, "What a dummy I am to have made *another* mistake!" By the time you think, "What a..." the typo is no more and the writing can continue.

Third of all, the more typing you do, the more familiar you become with the keyboard and the faster you type. Writing longhand is just the opposite. The more you write the more the hand tires and the slower you write.

I asked a friend for advice on whether I should spend my last dollar on a word processor. He recommended that I make two lists, one giving all the reasons I should buy a word processor and the other giving all the reasons I shouldn't. I sat down, pen in hand, and began listing. The "shouldn't" list began with "It costs a lot" and went on for about a third of a page. The "should" list continued for a page-and-a-half and ended with "No more cramped hands!" because, by the end of the second list, my hand was, indeed, cramped. I honestly think I spent $7,500 because of a cramped hand.

If you are a writer who is used to writing everything out longhand, adjusting to a keyboard and a video screen will take some time, but not as much as you may think. Before getting a word processor my standard method of writing was with pen on paper. I made corrections by crossing out and adding little " ^ " marks all over the place. I then turned this over to a typist with extreme patience and a working knowledge of hieroglyphics. I made further corrections on the typed copy.

(Things always look different when they're typed, don't they?) Then the typist retyped what I hoped would be the final copy.

It took me very little time to adjust to a keyboard and a screen. I can actually read what I've written as I write it; changes are simple; additions are included automatically as part of the text (if you've ever spent time following a string of " ⌃ s" around a hand-corrected page, you'll appreciate that feature); and the copy, as I enter it, looks typed right there on the video screen. In addition, there are no multiple trips to the typist.

If you know nothing about typing at all, your investment of time in learning how to use a word processor increases. If you take a decent touch-typing course (you can buy a program that uses your computer to teach you), within six months you'll be several steps ahead of us hunt-and-peck artists. (The tragedy of the hunt-and-peck boys and girls is that we know enough to get by, but we never learn the fastest way to type. Sigh.)

So, there are costs to word processing. They are: Time and Money.

Are those costs justified for your particular usage? For your particular situation, is it worth it? That depends. Rather than give a questionnaire ("On the average, how many words do you type each week?"), let me give some examples in which word processing would be most, and least, beneficial. You can then find your place along that continuum.

A person least benefited by a word processor would be a businessperson who dictates a few letters each week, all different; knows nothing about typing, spelling, grammar, or standard correspondence formats; and has a secretary who dutifully takes care of all that. Whether the *secretary* could benefit from a word processor is another question. Also another question is whether the businessperson would benefit from some other programs available for the personal computer — financial planning and the like. Would this person, who cannot type, who writes very little, get much use from a word processor? No. Hopefully, if this person should happen to get a computer, it should be equipped with a Space Invaders game so that he or she will be able to get some practical use from the machine.

The people who would benefit most from word processing are the secretary, especially one who deals with contracts or correspondence that repeat the same information over and over; the student, especially one with a heavy work load of book reports, term papers, and love letters; and the writer, especially one who demands letter-perfect copy, writes at hours — and on a budget — far too unpredictable to include a secretary, and who has a certain degree of correspondence to maintain.

If you fall into any of those three categories, make the obtaining of a word processor your top priority; it will change your life. Secretaries: leave a copy of this book open to the chapter **Word Processing in the Office** on your boss's desk or next to the coffee machine or in the executive washroom. Students: send a copy of this book, the chapter **Word Processing for Students** marked, along with a poorly-typed note to your parents, hinting strongly that the difference between the honor roll and dropping out lies in their hands. Writers: stop eating, write a quickie pornographic-science-fiction-horror-gothic-romance-thriller, become a gigolo; sell out in whatever way you may have remaining to get one of these things.

There is a middle ground — those people who live ordinary lives; who write a little or correspond a little; who have a portable typewriter sitting on its "free with purchase" typewriter table in that corner of the living room loosely referred to as "the office." What about those people? Again, it depends. Do you have a whole lot of money?

If you do, and if you have the time it takes to learn how to use it, then by all means get a word processor. If you don't have a lot of money, then to word process or not to word process will depend on how useful you would find the other capabilities of personal computers: balancing the family budget, educating the children, charting biorhythms, playing Star-Trek, and the many other wonders described in past and future issues of Popular Computing, BYTE, Interface Age, Personal Computing, Creative Computing, and other magazines and books on the subject.

A new newsletter on the subject might prove useful, especially if you're a writer. It's called *WP News: A Writer's*

POV on Word Processing. (POV is screenwriter talk for "point of view.") It costs $20 a year and includes hardware reviews, software reviews, and interviews with word processor users. If you'd like to subscribe, the address is in the back of this book.

You'll have to weigh the features and programs of personal computers in general until a critical mass is obtained and the scales tip in the direction of "Forget It" or "Go for It."

I am noticing that this chapter ends somewhat up in the air. I was fishing about for a sentence or two that might help ground it and realized that "up in the air" is where many people will be about word processing at this point. Those who have decided "No" found ample excuses not to read any further in the last chapter's list of drawbacks. Those who have decided "Yes" have skipped this chapter and are well into **Selecting a Word Processing Computer.**

I have no easy solutions to offer. It was eight months from the time I was first told about word processing computers until I finally purchased one. In that time I went from "I don't need one" to "I've got to have one" and back again several times. There were periods of intense research and times when the subject was forgotten. Obviously, I am thrilled with my final decision, but my situation and needs may be very different from yours.

The only thing I know to do during periods of indecision is to continue gathering information.

If you are in doubt as to how helpful word processing may be in your particular situation, you might try renting a word processor for a month or so and find out first hand. Look under office equipment rentals in the Yellow Pages.

Another suggestion is to visit a word processing center where computers are rented by the hour. We have one in Los Angeles called WordPlay. It's a sort of Romper Room for writers. Again, check the Yellow Pages under "Computers" or "Word Processing" or similar headings.

Read the next two chapters and make the rounds of the computer stores. Buy some computer magazines. Read some books on other features personal computers offer. You might want to try my friend's suggestion and make a list of the pros and a list of the cons for your particular situation. That helped clarify it for me.

And while you're up in the air, enjoy the view.

Here we have an early personal computer...

And the same computer as illustrated in Playboy.

Chapter Twelve

Selecting a Word Processing Computer

Let's assume you've decided to purchase a personal computer. Which one should you get? That depends on what you want to use the computer for.

If you want to use the computer for playing games, buy the best possible game-playing computer around. You may be able to patch together a semi-adequate word processing system from it. You want it primarily to educate the children? Then find out who offers the best educational software and buy a computer that will run it. Again, you'll no doubt be able to adapt that computer into a fairly decent word processing machine. You want it primarily for business? See answer to next question. You want to primarily process words? Then you have come to the right place.

You see, computers that play games very well process words rather poorly. In the first place, joysticks are utterly useless in the processing of words. A joystick is a little device you hold in your hand while playing a computer game. It tells the spaceship which way to go and when to fire. I always thought it would be fun to have a spaceship cruise through my text, shooting laser beams and exploding — with sound effects — unwanted text. This would be followed by a Writer's Sky Lab, from which little Authornauts descend, constructing the desired sentences.

Secondly, most good game computers use color video screens. This is great for Star Wars but bad for star writers. With few exceptions, the characters on a color video screen are not very sharp. This is especially true of computers that use a standard commercial color television for the video display. (Video monitors are much sharper than regular televisions.) This fuzziness of characters increases eyestrain and makes the editing process uncomfortable.

Thirdly, computers that handle graphics well, spaceships and alien invaders and the like, often do not do such a good job with words. This is because the operating system is designed for flashy graphics and not for words.

Not that word processing on a full-color, game-oriented computer is not possible; it is. In fact, you'll find word processing on all but the worst of the game computers several times easier and faster than even the best electric typewriters. It will not, however, be as easy or as enjoyable as processing words on a computer designed for processing words.

Educational computers for children generally fall into the game-computer category. Color graphics hold a child's attention longer than black-and-white words. The same limitations in terms of fuzzy character display applies.

Computers for educating older students and adults often use words rather than graphics. These programs are usually designed or available for computers that are also great for word processing.

Computers used for business applications generally have the same objectives as word processing computers: comfortable, no-nonsense entry of text and figures; crisp, sharp display of letters and numbers.

Hence, if you are primarily purchasing a computer for games, color graphics such as a video artist would use, or the education of younger children, the computer you'll need to buy will do word processing, but you will not have an optimal word processor. If, however, business, accounting, adult education, and word processing are your primary uses for a computer, read on. What to look for in the purchase of this kind of computer is what we'll examine next.

For those who will be using a computer almost exclusively for word processing, the question often arises: "Should I buy a personal computer with a word processing program or should I buy a specially designed word processing machine?"

Computers designed for word processing only are known as **dedicated** word processors. They are sold by big computer companies to other big companies for big prices. The dollar-for-dollar value of these dedicated units, when compared with regular, programmable personal computers, is low. But even big businesses are getting wise and more and more "economy" versions of these ten-to-twenty-thousand-dollar profit-makers are being introduced by the computer giants.

For under $7,000 you can have every feature available from a $10,000 to $20,000 dedicated word processor but two:

(1) a Bigtime computer nameplate and (2) a handsome salesman or beautiful saleswoman to hold your hand while you learn the intricacies of word processing. For $3,000 to $13,000 you can buy a great many name plates and an awful lot more than hand holding.

Further, you are bound to the features of that word processor and are at the mercy of the Big Computer Company to make improvements on your system.

Furthermore, if you want to do anything on the machine other than process words, you can't. What you wanted was a word processor and what you got was a word processor. You want to balance your checkbook? Buy our dedicated Checkbook Balancer.

I am not, by the way, referring to the new personal computers that IBM and Xerox and a few of the other big companies are coming out with. These are computers that are competitively priced and allow a great many different programs to be run on them. I am speaking of $10,000-and-up dedicated word processors. Dedicated word processors are dedicated to the proposition that big businesses don't know the meaning of value when it comes to word processing computers.

In looking for a personal computer to be used for word processing, some features are more important than others. Here is a list of them in order of importance.

THE PROGRAM

In selecting a word processor, the first and most important consideration is the software or word processing program. It must do all that you want it to do.

You can use the listing of features in *Chapter Three*, **The Wonders of Word Processing**, to help you decide what you want or need. Explore how various software programs operate and what they offer. You can purchase the software manuals, also known as **documentation**, to most programs without buying the program. These cost about ten percent of the program's total cost. The manual for a $500 program might cost you $50. If you're shopping at a friendly computer or software store, they might loan you several manuals for a few days. Reading the manuals of three or four word processing programs will give you an excellent basis from which to choose the program that's right for you.

Start with the software you like best with the features you want most and build your word processing system around it.

Before you can run a word processing program on your personal computer, you must run another program before it. This program is known as the Disk Operating System (DOS), and it tells the computer how to store and retrieve information from the disks. As mentioned before, the standard for personal computers used for nongraphic applications is a Disk Operating System known as CP/M. CP/M is short for Control Program for Microcomputers or Control Program Monitor, depending upon which book you read.

Most of the powerful word processing programs require CP/M. CP/M also allows you to take advantage of a great many business related programs. CP/M is the most popular disk operating system for nongame-oriented personal computers.

THE KEYBOARD AND VIDEO SCREEN

The second most important part of your word processing computer is the keyboard and the video screen. Together they are known as a terminal. The terminal is where you'll spend most of your time: looking at the video screen, tapping on the keyboard. You must feel totally comfortable with both.

The screen should display characters that are crisp and sharp and clear. Characters are formed on the video screen by little dots. The more little dots, the sharper the character. These are usually referred to as "character dot matrix" or "character formation resolution" or some such jargon. In the specifications it will list how many dots horizontally and how many dots vertically make up a letter. "6 x 8" or "7 x 10" or "14 x 10" are ways in which they're listed. The higher the numbers, the better.

Then there is the question of how many characters fit

on a line and how many lines are displayed on the screen. Low-rent screens will give you 64 characters and 16 lines, or less. Better terminals will display 80 characters and 24 lines. Twenty-four lines is about half a typewritten page, and it's plenty. It shows enough of what has gone on before and if you need to review, **scrolling** to another part of the text is fast and easy. (Scrolling refers to moving forward or backward in a document. The idea is that the text is written on an imaginary scroll, the two rolls of which are just above and just below the video screen.)

Screens that display full pages of text (55 lines or so) are hindrances. Tests have shown that the operator spends a great deal of time actually touching the screen to hold a place because too much information is being displayed at one time.

Green phosphor is supposed to be easier on the eyes than standard black and white. I really don't know. My suggestion is to use both a black and white and a green phosphor video screen for a while to see which one you prefer. If you decide to get a green screen, make sure the actual *phosphor* is green, not just a black and white screen with a piece of green plastic over it. There are also amber phosphor screens that someone described to me as "better than sex." I doubt it. The only thing I have found that's better than sex is chocolate chip cookies.

The keyboard should be a standard typewriter keyboard. The letters should be large and the keys slightly curved like little dishes, not flat. This curve fits the curve of the fingertip. A numeric keypad, a rectangle of keys to the right of the regular keyboard with the numbers 0 through 9 laid out like a calculator, is a must if you work with numbers.

As you hit a letter you should not hear a plastic "ping" or "click" echoing through the keyboard. A keyboard that sounds cheap will produce cheap writing. It's a psychological fact. Most of all, *you* must enjoy typing on it. Not unlike Fairy Princes and Princesses, there are a great many keyboards out there. Try them all until you find the one you fall in love with.

I recommend detachable keyboards wholeheartedly. Some computers have the keyboard cemented to the video screen. Other computers have the keyboard on a cord so that the keyboard can be over here and over here and over here and over here and the video screen remains over there.

I have become quite attached to my detachable keyboard. I can lean back in my chair, cross my legs, put the keyboard on my lap and write, write, write. When editing I place the keyboard closer to the video screen so that I can see the text more clearly. Thus far I have never had to get as close to the video screen as I would have if the keyboard were permanently attached to it. This allows for less eyestrain, and if there is any radiation coming from the video screen, the video screen is over there and I'm over here.

The variety of positions permitted with a detachable keyboard is invaluable during long hours of writing. I know someone who does it while lying flat on his waterbed. I haven't gone quite that far — I don't like waterbeds — but it's nice to know that the possibility exists. It's also great when copying text from another written source. The original can go between the keyboard and the video screen. One need only look up-and-down, not left-to-right-and-up-and-down: Much easier, and much less strain on the neck, shoulders, and spine. Sitting in a twisted position for long periods of time is not known for its life enhancing qualities.

Ask the manufacturer of the software you've chosen for a list of computers that work best with their word processing program. Some computers will allow you to move the cursor about the screen using little arrows, others require depressing a "control" button with one hand while pressing a letter with the other. Although the control/letter method of moving the cursor around is easily adjusted to, many prefer using separate cursor movement keys.

THE PRINTER

The next consideration is that of a printer. There are two kinds, dot matrix and letter quality. Dot matrix printers cost less to buy and print faster, yet the quality of the printed text, while readable, leaves much to be desired. Letter quality printers cost more to buy and print more slowly, but the quality of their finished pages rivals that of the best electric typewriters.

Which is best for word processing? Clearly, letter

quality. Correspondence, manuscripts, term papers — almost anything but in-house financial statements and invoices — look unbearably chintzy when printed on a dot matrix printer.

But which letter quality printer? There are basically three kinds: converted IBM Selectrics, daisy wheel, and thimble. The IBM Selectrics print slowly, about 15 characters per second (CPS), and will not do all the things daisy wheel or thimble printers will, such as bold face printing. Also, they may require more servicing than do daisy wheel or thimble printers. Converted Selectrics, however, when properly adjusted, do produce excellent-quality printing and can be purchased fairly inexpensively.

Daisy wheel printers are so named because the printing element is a metal or plastic circle with "petals" Salvador Dali might mistake for a flower. Similarly, thimble printers use a print element that resembles a thimble, providing that the tip of one's finger is two inches wide. (Who names these things anyway?)

Metal daisy wheels give better print quality than do plastic daisy wheels, but plastic wheels print faster than metal ones. Thimble printers combine maximum speed (55 characters per second, or about 450 words per minute) with maximum print quality. Thimble printers tend to be slightly more expensive than their daisy wheel cousins.

If money is a major factor in your decision, you can save quite a bit of it by buying a daisy wheel or thimble printer that prints at 25 or 35 CPS rather than at 55 CPS. Everything will take about twice as long to print, but you'll initially save almost $1,000.

DISK DRIVES AND DISK SIZE

The next items to be considered are disks and disk drives. Are disk drives necessary for word processing? No. Are they necessary for any serious word processing? Yes. What's "serious?" Anything more than a two-or three-page letter is serious. Any major block moves or file insertions are serious. The desire for even moderate speed and accuracy is serious. In other words, if you want your word processor to write something more significant than an occasional letter to Mother, you'll need a disk drive.

Not only do disk drives allow for maximum flexibility with the material you create, they also allow your computer to take advantage of the finest software. The most powerful programs are generally available only on disks and require at least one disk drive to operate.

The question then arises: How many disk drives do you need? The answer: You can get by with one, but you'll be a lot happier with two.

In the first place, with two drives you'll have more "on line" storage. This means that your files, hence your documents, can be longer; you can store dozens of extra "boilerplate" paragraphs which can be inserted into letters, contracts and manuscripts; and you can have more programs on line so that you can work on one file with several programs — text editing followed by spelling checking followed by word counting, for example.

Secondly, and perhaps most importantly, with two disk drives copying files and disks is a breeze. Copying is an essential part of computerized word processing just as copying is an essential part of any office. (What ever did the world do before Xerox machines?) Copying is used to create disks upon which files can then be written, moving files from one disk to one or several others, and making back-up copies.

Back-up copies of files, and even whole disks, are vitally important. Because hundreds of pages of text can be stored on just one disk, if anything should happen to that precious disk — from a cup of spilled coffee to a disk-hungry computer — it's spelled C-A-T-A-S-T-R-O-P-H-E. If you've been a good word processing operator and have made a back-up copy of that disk a short while before, that's spelled R-E-L-I-E-F. Copying whole disks with two disk drives takes minutes. With only one disk drive it takes much, much longer and, in some cases, is not possible.

The next question about disk drives: Should they be 8-inch or 5¼-inch? Eight-inch disks hold more information but they cost more to buy and are more cumbersome to work with. Five-and-a-quarter inch disks potentially hold less information than do 8-inch disks, but they cost less and are easier to work with when changing disks. Further, 5¼-inch disks are far more popular in the personal computer world than 8-inch disks. The opposite is true in the world of small business computers.

Your choice of 5¼ vs 8-inch will depend largely on how much storage you will need at any one time. As mentioned before, the amount of information stored on a disk is measured in Kilobytes, or "Ks." Each "K" is equal to 1,024 letters, numbers or spaces. A typewritten, double-spaced 8½ x 11 sheet of paper with generous margins contains approximately 2K of information. You can use this as a good rule of thumb when deciding how much disk storage you'll need.

Fortunately, floppy disks are more compact than they were several years ago.

What is the longest continuous document you will regularly use your word processor to edit? Find out how many "K" that would be, multiply by three, and that will give you the approximate disk size needed for each of your two disk drives.

For example, if your longest continuous document is about 25 double-spaced, typewritten pages, that is around 50K (2K per page). 50K tripled is 150K. Hence you will need two disk drives with storage of at least 150K each.

Why triple? Most quality word processing programs automatically make a back-up copy of each file you work on. This is a safety measure so that if you royally mess up the second time through a document, you will have a copy of the first time to fall back on. This feature is rarely needed but when it is, it's worth its weight in microprocessor-grade silicon. It does, however, mean that a 50K file, when backed up, will take 100K of disk space.

Okay, that's double. Why triple? Safety. Margin for error. Buffer zone. That sort of thing. Many word processing programs add little formatting codes that, although invisible on the video screen, do add a "K" here and a "K" there to disk storage space. Also you never know when you'll want to do a 30-page file, and there is nothing more frightening than having an absolute masterpiece in the memory of the computer, and right in the middle of transferring it to the permanency of a disk have the video screen signal DISK FULL. Well, just put in a new disk, you say. Alas, it's not always that easy. (There are usually solutions, and they differ from program to program.)

When I say "continuous file," I mean a document in which you need to do a great deal of moving information within the document. A continuous file need not be the length of an entire book, for example. The length of an average chapter or even a section within a chapter may be all the file space you'll need. Each chapter or section can be stored on separate disks.

Five-and-a-quarter inch disks are easier to manipulate than their eight-inch siblings. Not only are eight inch disks larger, they also tend to sag and bend more easily. Unless you need the massive storage capabilities of eight-inch disks, you may be happier with five-and-a-quarter.

Before we leave disks, a word about hard disks. Hard disks hold huge amounts of information and are hugely expensive. For most word processing applications you will not need a hard disk — putting your information on a series of floppy disks and changing disks when the information is needed will usually suffice. Hard disks would be needed, for example, in legal departments, where hundreds and hundreds of boilerplate paragraphs must be accessed continuously in the writing of contracts; or when there are thousands of names on a mailing list and the operator must refer to them frequently. Hard disks are used more often for data processing than for word processing.

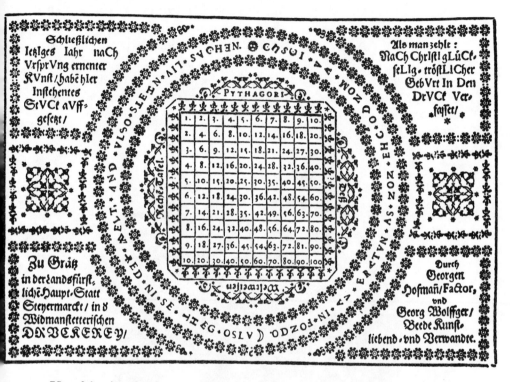

Use this simple chart to help you decide how much disk capacity you'll need.

THE COMPUTER

Ironically enough, the least important consideration in the selection of a word processing computer is the computer itself. Most top-quality word processing and business programs require computers with a Z80 Central Processing Unit (CPU) and a CP/M Disk Operating System (DOS). Z80 and CP/M have become industry standards for personal computers used for nongame applications. I once had the misfortune of playing Space Invaders on a Z80, CP/M system. Dull. Slow. It was like those nightmares in which you're the welfare budget and you're being chased by Ronald Reagan. Awful.

CP/M can also run on 8080 and 8085 Central Processing Units. There are some very good computers coming out that use 8086 and 8088 microprocessors. If the program you've chosen will run on these, fine.

The RAM you will need will vary depending upon the software you select. It will no doubt be between 32K and 64K. It is rare that you'll need more than 64K of RAM. (Remember that in better word processing programs the size of your document is limited to the size of your *disk* capacity and not your RAM capacity.)

"Word Processing is here, tra la."

What, then, would be the specifications of a personal computer that would be used almost exclusively for word processing; a word processor that would do the job, but not overdo it? The following is my list of recommended specifications:

Word Processing Program: One that will do everything you want it to do.

Dictionary Program: The WORD or The WORD PLUS by Oasis Systems.

Video Screen: Black and white or green phosphor. (Not color.) Clear, sharp, easily readable characters. 24 lines, each line being 80 characters in length.

Keyboard: Detachable. Large letters. Good, solid, comfortable feel. No plastic-sounding "clickety-clicks." Keys slightly concave.

Printer: Letter quality. Thimble.

Disk Drives: Two. 5¼ inch. 150K to 340K each.

Disk Operating System (DOS): CP/M.

Central Processing Unit (CPU): Z80, 8080, 8085, 8086 or 8088. Choose the one that works best with your software.

Random Access Memory (RAM): 48K to 64K.

Scotch: Dewar's White Label.

Chapter Thirteen

A Brand Name Buying Guide

In this chapter we'll look at some of the most popular personal computers, printers, and word processing software. The question is not "Which one is a good computer?" since all the computers listed in this chapter are "good." The questions we'll be asking are "Which personal computers make the best word processors?" and "Which personal computers do the most for the least amount of money?"

This chapter is up-to-date until May 1, 1983. If you are buying a computer after that time, please drop me a note and ask for Update #4. Things change quickly in the world of personal computers, and I'm sure you'll want to make you're choice with full knowledge of these changes. My address is at the end of this chapter.

I enjoy recommending things to people, but in the world of personal computers things change too quickly to make static recommendations. Books last *a long time*, and to list the best personal computers for word processing is not as safe as, say, recommending the world's most beautiful waterfalls.

The Update, then, bridges the gap between the permanency of the printed page and the ongoingness of the computer industry. I shudder to think, for example, that someone would go out and buy an Osborne 1 based upon the first edition of this book, never knowing about the KayComp II (now called the KayPro II), discussed in the second edition. (Also in Update #1.)

I imagine that sooner or later I will be issuing an annual edition of this book, like *Consumer Report* Buying Guides, Guinness Book of World Records, or Fodor's Travel Guides. Maybe I'll become like the auto manufacturers, issuing "1984½" models.

A few people have written (by far the minority) *outraged* that I did not cover this-or-that computer, *demanding* that I redeem myself by giving a full report by return mail.

There are over 200 personal computers on the market, with more being introduced every day. I will never be able to review them all. By the time I reviewed the 200, there would be 200 more, then I would have to go back and start over, covering improvements on the original 200. It is an endless task.

My criteria for choosing computers, programs, and peripherals to review are simple.

First, I try to evaluate machines that are widely advertised and widely available. Some make poor word processors (Apple and Atari) and some make great word processors (IBM and DEC). I feel it's as important to steer people *away* from heavily-advertised poor values as it is to steer them *toward* not-so-heavily-advertised better values.

Which brings us to the second criterion: value. If a small company is turning out a product of exceptional value, I tend to gravitate towards that. I don't think anyone reading **The Word Processing Book** could have missed my admiration for The Word Plus. It is still not only the best spell-check program but, at $150, the best *value* in spell-check programs available today.

A third criterion is simply what people ask about. Although I keep no scientific records, I'm sure that a subconscious counter is clicking away the number of times people write asking about this computer or that program.

The fourth criterion is uniqueness. *The* most portable computer, or the *only* word processing program designed especially for screenwriters is likely to attract my attention.

The fifth criterion is price. I have arbitrarily decided to review computers costing $5,000 or less (not including printer or software). There is plenty of word processing power in the under-$5,000 category, and to go over that takes one into the world of *mini*-computers, which is another world entirely. Hence, I will not be reviewing the Fortune 32:16 or the new Corvus.

The sixth criterion is versatility. The machines should be able to do something other than word processing. I therefore stay away from "dedicated" or "stand alone" word processors. These machines (Lanier, Wang, IBM Display Writer) are utterly dependent upon the host company for revision, improvement, and expansion. Besides, they usually cost over $5,000.

The seventh criterion is screen and keyboard. An eighty-character screen and a detachable keyboard are so valuable for word processing — and there are so many wonderful, inexpensive personal computers that feature both — I tend to avoid personal computers that do not have them.

The final criterion is simply my own personal interests. I'm a lousy speller and spend no time footnoting, so I tend to pay more attention to spell-check programs than I do to footnote programs. I cannot pretend that *all* my criteria are objective. Frankly, I'm not sure if any of them are.

My hope is that, between **The Word Processing Book**, **The Personal Computer Book**, and comments in the buying guide, I will help to create educated consumers: people who will be able to look at computers and decide for themselves whether those machines would make good word processors or not. (Well, I can *hope*, can't I?)

* * * *

Let's look first at software, then at printers and finally at personal computers themselves.

SOFTWARE

The two most popular word processing programs for personal computers are WordStar and PeachText (formerly Magic Wand). In terms of sales and popularity, WordStar has the edge. Both are fine programs and each has its strengths and weaknesses. In general, WordStar's strengths lie in the area of editing and PeachText's strengths lie in the area of printing.

WordStar

If one had to choose an industry standard for word processing software it would be WordStar. All the features listed in *Chapter Three*, **The Wonders of Word Processing** are included with WordStar except a dictionary program, proportional spacing and kerning.

WordStar is a screen oriented program. What you see on the video screen is exactly the way the text will appear when printed, word for word, line for line, page for page.

Giving commands to WordStar one uses a standard key on all personal computers, the **control key**. With the control key depressed all the characters on the keyboard take on a new meaning. It's rather like sending your keyboard to est. The control key is depressed and, while depressed, one or two other keys are hit. In this way WordStar uses a standard keyboard to communicate 97 different commands.

If you were to type "KY," one would think you were discussing a lubricating jelly. If you type "KY" while depressing the control key, you would be telling WordStar that you wanted a certain block of text deleted. (The computer abbreviation for the control key is "^"."^KY" or "Control-KY" both mean "Depress the control key and hit "KY.")

To move the cursor, for example, you would press ^ E, ^ S, ^ D, or ^ X. The letters E, S, D and X form a diamond on the keyboard: E is on top, S is left, D is right and X is down. Hence, with WordStar, if you want to move the cursor up the screen you would press ^ E. If you wanted to move it left you would press^ S. If you wanted to move it right you would press ^ D, and ^ X would move it down. Typists can do this with one hand, usually. The control key is located close to the E-S-D-X diamond on the keyboard. Hunt-and-peckers such as myself will find that two hands are necessary. (Some computers, such as Xerox, Otrona, and Osborne, have adapted WordStar so that cursor movement keys move the cursor.)

^ KB marks the beginning of a block of type; ^ KK marks the end. ^ KV moves the marked block to another part of the text. ^ OR sets the right margin, ^ OL sets the left. ^ G deletes a character,^ T deletes a word,^ Y deletes a whole line, and so on.

All this might seem confusing at first and rather hard to learn. Why not have some extra keys on the keyboard with those functions clearly labeled? Surely pressing a "Delete Character" key is easier than remembering "^ G." So it seems, but keep in mind that you would need a keyboard with at least 97 extra keys, all with little printing on them, saying things like "Save, exit to operating system," or "Read file into text." This would not only add to the cost, as it does with stand alone word processors, but it would also add to the confusion.

Further, once you know that ^ G means "delete

character" it's much faster to find ˆ G than a new key labeled "delete character." This is because a typist — even a poor one like me — already knows where "G" is. One need only learn the placement of one new key, the control key. It is easier for the mind to learn that "ˆ G equals delete character" than it is for the hand to learn the placement of a delete character key.

This is one reason programs that are advertised as "easy to learn" should be examined carefully. Programs that are easy to learn are often difficult to use. Imagine riding a bicycle on which the training wheels were never removed.

WordStar has a companion program, MailMerge, that is highly recommended if you want to print form letters or multiple copies of the same document.

WordStar is the product that put its manufacturer, MicroPro International, on the map. It is well supported, although in recent months they seem to be spending their corporate time developing programs that imitate existing programs from other manufacturers rather than keeping WordStar the best. They released, for example, a truly mediocre spelling program, SpellStar, rather than adding proportional spacing, footnoting, and other potential improvements to WordStar. It is doubtful, however, that they will ever let WordStar slip too far behind the competition.

PeachText

Magic Wand, a good and popular program, was purchased about a year ago by Peachtree Software, manufacturer of a line of business software that is highly respected in the industry. (IBM chose the Peachtree line of business software for their Personal Computer.)

Peachtree spent the first year removing bugs from Magic Wand and improving one of Magic Wand's primary claims to fame: proportional spacing. Then they changed the name to PeachText. Peachtree is a bright, assertive company and the future of PeachText looks good.

PeachText currently features all the capabilities listed in Chapter Three except a dictionary, page break display, double strike and strikeout (no loss there).

PeachText is a character-oriented word processing

program. This means that what you see on the screen has no relation to what will be printed on paper, except that one word will follow another and sentences and paragraphs will begin as indicated. There is no way of knowing where pages will break, for example, without a test print-out.

When you buy PeachText it is customized for your keyboard. In this way cursor movement keys (these are keys with little arrows pointing up, down, left and right) can be used. PeachText makes maximum use of special function keys as well.

The manual is presented in a lesson-by-lesson logical format. This, too, has been one of the traditional strengths of Magic Wand.

The print functions on PeachText are very powerful. In addition to the aforementioned proportional spacing, Peach-Text supports nine — count 'em, nine — intensities of bold face printing.

This is level one.
This is level two.
This is level three.
This is level four.
This is level five.
This is level six.
This is level seven.
This is level eight.
This is level nine.

PeachText also does kerning, which will move a single character a fraction of a millimeter to the right or to the left within a word on the printed page.

Unfortunately, PeachText does not have one of the simplest print commands, print pause. This would allow one to change print wheels to, say, italicize certain words. Double strike would also be useful for some typesetting situations.

PeachText allows for a choice when printing with justified right hand margins: microspacing (spacing between letters) or regular spacing (spaces placed between words only). Although microspacing looks better, tests indicate that regular spacing is easier to read.

Another interesting feature is Flush Right-
Ragged Left. Since Flush Left-Ragged Right is the
accepted standard for correspondence, sending out your letters
with ragged left margins give your missives that style, that
flair, that air of well-modulated independence that will make
them truly noticed or truly ignored. If you haven't already
guessed, this paragraph is using Flush Right-Ragged Left
margins.

As you can see, neither is the perfect program. One wishes in that moment between sleeping and waking, when the impossible becomes possible and all dreams come true, that MicroPro and Peachtree would join forces as Microtree or PeachPro and, taking the best from their respective programs, create WordText or PeachStar — Super Software that would help writers, secretaries and students everywhere in our never ending battle for truth, justice and the American way.

Easy Writer II

When IBM was selecting software to offer with their personal computer, they chose a program from Information Unlimited Software called Easy Writer that had been quite popular on the Apple. One does not know quite why IBM made this choice, but it was clearly the weakest link in their personal computer offering. (That and the placement of the shift key, which we'll discuss later.)

Critics of Easy Writer who were kind dubbed it Not-So-Easy Writer. Critics who were less kind called it Sleazy Writer. The word went out: If you buy the IBM Personal Computer, don't buy Easy Writer with it.

Into this maelstrom of bad publicity comes Information Unlimited Software (IUS) with a new word processing program, Easy Writer II. Easy Writer II is an excellent program, light years removed from Easy Writer 1. If you hear discussions about Easy Writer, make sure you ask if they mean Easy Writer 1 (now owned by IBM) or Easy Writer II. In this chapter I will be discussing Easy Writer II.

Easy Writer II is designed especially for the IBM Personal Computer. It will only run on the IBM, therefore if you want this program, you must also get an IBM.

Easy Writer II has a few features not available on either PeachText or WordStar (thus far. Keep in mind that serious word processing on personal computers has only been around for three-or-so years and that updates on software — like new editions of a book — are continually being released. These updates are available for a small portion of the purchase price, usually $15 to $35.)

One such EasyWriter II feature, invaluable to screen-writers, is the ability to switch from one preset margin to another to another. Easy Writer II does this with three keystrokes and a return. The program will memorize up to eight preset margins.

(Aside to screenwriters: Keep in mind that almost any program will print proper script formats. With Word-Star, for example, you can center a character's name with three keystrokes, then type out action and dialog using the margins for action. The margins can then be reset — seven keystrokes to reset both left and right margins — and the dialog can be reformed, speech by speech. This is easier than it sounds, but not as easy as pushing one button and having all margins automatically reset — a feature that is currently available only on far more expensive stand-alone word processors.)

In addition to margins, EasyWriter II will also mem-orize other formatting commands such as decimal tabs, character pitch, and line spacing.

EasyWriter II is a screen oriented program — what you see on the screen is what you'll see on the paper. This is more true of EasyWriter II than with any other program I know. Since it's written especially for the IBM, words that are underlined display on the video screen as underlined, words that are in bold display in bold. (With other word processing programs, one puts what are known as **embedded commands** into the text. These display on the screen before and after the highlighted area. For example, if you wanted to print the word "word" in boldface, the screen on WordStar would display ˆ Bwordˆ B. In PeachText it would display @word@.

These embedded text commands can be switched off so that they will not display in WordStar. They cannot be switched off in PeachText.)

A drawback of EasyWriter II is that it does not store text in standard CP/M files, therefore the text can only be worked on by programs furnished by Information Unlimited Software. You could not, for example, use The WORD Plus to check the spelling of a document. (IUS offers a very good spell-check program called EasySpeller, although it's not as good as The WORD Plus.) It is not even certain that you can use text manipulation programs written especially for the IBM. (Some work, and some do not.)

The reasons for all this are given later in the chapter when I discuss the IBM Personal Computer. Keep in mind that what you gain in features you may lose in flexibility.

In all, though, EasyWriter II is a fine word processing program, well worthy of your consideration.

The EasyWriter II people have added a unique level of support to their software. For 20% of the purchase price (about $70 for EasyWriter II) you get unlimited use of a toll-free help line for one full year. This is invaluable when learning a program. Let's hope more software houses follow Information Unlimited's lead. IUS has also introduced EasyFiler, a sophisticated filing system that interfaces with EasyWriter II.

Volkswriter

This is a new, inexpensive ($195) word processing program written especially for the IBM Personal Computer. While I have not had a chance to evaluate it, it is getting a good reputation among IBMophiles.

Select

Select is a program that is easy to learn, but cumbersome to use. Further, it doesn't begin to approach the power of, say, WordStar.

The strength of Select is an excellent interactive tutorial that comes with each program. This tutorial takes a person in gradual and enjoyable steps through the various features of the program. The "student" is encouraged to "give it a try" each step of the way. If one accomplishes the task correctly the student is rewarded with, "WOW! Am I impressed!" or "You're HOT!" If one fails, however, he or she is chided with, "Have you ever felt like the ship was sailing without you? Please go back and give it one more try." or "If you can't get this one you're looking out the window."

Using this tutorial, within an hour or so one could be successfully processing words using Select.

The problem comes after you've used Select continuously for several weeks. Select is what I call a **multi-screen program**. This means that you enter text on one screen, then must switch screens to do any editing of the entered text. If you've typed a sentence, look at it on the screen, and see that a letter needs replacing, rather than simply going back to that letter and changing it, you must exit the "text entry" screen and enter the "edit" screen. After the correction has been made, you must exit the edit screen and once again return to the text entry screen.

Select is rather like a tool kit with lots and lots of easy to learn tools and a jolly Mr. Goodwrench to teach you how to use them. If you use tools infrequently, this will serve you well. If you use tools often, the bending and reaching and constant manipulation of tools can become annoying.

Select is a great word processing program for those who do little word processing. It's easy to learn and easy to relearn. And if you only use a hammer to pound a few tacks every week, you'll never find yourself longing for a hydraulic staple gun.

Scriptsit II

Whereas WordStar is difficult to learn but easy to use and Select is easy to learn but difficult to use, Scriptsit II is difficult to learn and difficult to use.

Scriptsit II is a multi-screen program and can be run only on Radio Shack computers. The files are not CP/M but TRSDOS (Tandy Radio Shack Disk Operating

System). This means that the text can only be manipulated with programs written for Radio Shack computers. It is even more cumbersome to operate than Select and at least as difficult to learn as WordStar.

Despite its many drawbacks it does offer a few features that most word processing programs do not, among them proportional spacing, margin memory (see EasyWriter II above), and a phrase storer. (The latter stores phrases that can later be added to the text.)

If you already have a Radio Shack computer, Scriptsit II might be a good choice. If you do not, it does not come highly recommended. (See comments about Radio Shack computers later in this chapter.)

Perfect Writer

Let us begin by accepting the fact that there *is* no perfect word processing program. Word processing is still dominated by tradeoffs ("In order to have this you can't have that") and personal tastes (some people like pushing special buttons to implement commands, others like a control key followed by a familiar character on the keyboard).

Perfection, in fact, is probably impossible. Like audio, state-of-the-art is the most one can hope for.

Is Perfect Writer, then, at least a state-of-the-art Writer? Well, it's headed in the right direction. Let's hope the creator(s) of this program do not take the program's name too much to heart: it is, by definition, impossible to improve upon perfection.

Perfect Writer has some useful features not offered by, say, WordStar. You can split the screen and edit two files simultaneously, moving text from one file to another if you like. It does true proportional spacing. It creates indexes and handles complicated footnoting.

It is not, however, a true screen-oriented program. Because it offers so many print and formatting options, what you see on the screen is not necessarily what you'll get on the printed page.

The documentation is excellent, the finest I have

read. Clear, well-illustrated, understandable, with occasional flashes of — would you believe it? — humor.

It is a first-rate program, one worthy of your careful consideration.

Spellbinder

Contrary to its name, Spellbinder is not a spell-check program. It is, in fact, a word processing program, and a good one too.

Like PeachText, the strength of Spellbinder lies in its printing. True proportional spacing, even typesetting printers (like the Sanders) are fully supported. (Oddly enough, as powerful as its printing capabilities are, it will not underline *and* boldface, or doublestrike *and* underline at the same time.)

Whenever a word processing program is powerful in printing, it usually sacrifices something in editing. The most obvious sacrifice is the lack of screen orientation. What you see on the screen while you're editing is not what you're likely to get on the paper. A preview mode, however, allows you to see how the text will look before it is printed, but to make any changes you must exit the preview mode and re-enter the edit mode. The what-you-see-is-what-you-get-while-editing feature is more important to some than to others.

Another editing weakness is the inability to insert while inserting. If you were, for example, inserting the line "We all had a nice day," and decided to back up and add "very" before "nice," you could not do it. You would have to leave the insert mode, return to the edit mode, move the cursor to the space before "nice," go back to the insert mode, and add "very."

In a sense, Spellbinder is a two-screen program, although not as cumbersome to use as, say, Select.

While we're on the subject of possible (I say possible because you might not mind any of these) drawbacks, managing very large files (files larger than the RAM of the computer) is less transparent than it is in, say, WordStar. For most letters, chapters, and articles, this will not pose a problem. For managing large mailing lists, it might be difficult. (I have mailing lists on a hard disk computer that are more than 400K. The computer itself has 64K on RAM, and editing large mailing lists like that would not be a simple task with Spellbinder. You cannot, for example, scroll backwards through a long file.)

Now the good stuff, and the reasons why some people think that Spellbinder is the best word processor around. To begin with, Spellbinder will (with the above exceptions) do everything listed in the chapter on **The Wonders of Word Processing**. Spellbinder is installed to use the function keys of most keyboards. Cursor movement keys move the cursor, and the computer takes on a more stand-alone word processor feel.

Spellbinder also has something known as *macros*. Macros are mini-programs that can be invoked with a keystroke or two. They allow the program to perform complicated, individualized functions with a minimum of effort. Because it's a program within a program, a macro provides specific customization and allows a wide variety of uses. (All those "special case" things you need to have done that no other word processor offers, you might be able to do with Spellbinder — but make sure it can before you buy.)

Although macros are a marvelous concept, I wish Spellbinder had a more structured way of "selling" them. Some dealers know how to write them, many don't. Simple macros can be gotten by calling Spellbinder's customer support department. There is no system for having complex micros written. Several popular macros are included with the program (some of them discussed below). A disk of the most frequently requested macros, and a system (so much per hour of programming time, for example) for customized macro writing would be a real plus.

Among the useful print options is the ability to print directly from the screen. With most word processing programs, the text must be saved on a disk and the file then printed from the disk. This is not much of an effort, but for labels, memos, and notes, direct printing from the screen is a convenience.

The supplied macros with Spellbinder include form generation and mail list management functions (alphabetizing, sorting by zip code, and so on) that many will find useful.

Also supplied are a variety of math functions (figures can be added across rows or down columns), and fixed point arithmetic.

In all, it's a powerful program worthy of your consideration.

Scriptor

Another program I have not seen is Scriptor. It is written with the screenwriter in mind. It formats text created with any CP/M-based word processing program to any of the various script formats. Were I a screen writer, I would certainly investigate this program.

Grammatik

This is a remarkable program that flags possible grammar and punctuation errors and even makes suggestions for correcting them. The effectiveness of Grammatik (pronounced gra-MAH-tic, as in "grammatical" without the "al") surprised me.

The text of this book has gone through two professional copy editors, two nonprofessional (though nonetheless paid) ones, two nonprofessional nonpaid ones, my mother and myself. In addition, letters from kindly strangers pointing out errors in the first edition of this book were duly massaged into the text. And along came Grammatik.

I thought it might be cute if a computer program found a mistake or two in the book. Cute? This thing is vicious. Not since Freshman Comp has my writing been so marked-up and questioned. Actually I didn't mind — much. I was, in fact, amazed and delighted and only occasionally defensive.

It began in the third paragraph of Chapter One. It suggested putting a question mark inside a set of quotation marks. It was right.

Then it picked apart the beginning of the fourth

paragraph, "In the last five years all of this has changed." It claimed that "all of this" is a wordy phrase and suggested that I simply use "all this." Again, it was right. "In the last five years all this has changed." is a better sentence.

Then it pointed out a misuse of "a while." (Should have been "awhile.") It said, "referred to as" is a wordy phrase and suggested "called." It recommended that I drop "of the envelope" in the sentence, "I must have received dozens of these, proclaiming on the outside of the envelope..." Again, it was right.

It pointed out that I am addicted to the word "very." Each time the word came up it was flagged for being a "vague adverb." I must have removed 30 "verys" from this book. It also flagged "upon," telling me it was "archaic." Well, my dictionary says it is "infrequently used" not "archaic," and I like it better than "on," so dozens of "upons" remain.

It tagged Xerox and Coke, told me they were trademarks, and suggested "photocopy" and "cola." (I like Xerox and Coke.) It said the phrase "reason why" was redundant which, of course, it is. It found a double "the" in a sentence ("it tells you that the the word...") that escaped everyone else. And on and on and on. Grammatik is responsible for more than fifty improvements in this book.

It was fun, though, to catch the taskmaster at its own task. It flagged the word "sort of" and labeled it a "wordy phrase." It suggested using either "somewhat" or "rather." If, however, one were to use "rather," it would later be tagged by Grammatik as a "vague adverb."

Grammatik is available with or without a spell-check program. Although its spell-check program is good, The WORD Plus is better.

Grammatik is available for Radio Shack, IBM and all CP/M computers. It costs $150.

Punctuation and Style

An even better program for checking punctuation and grammar is the latest brainchild from the creator of The Word Plus, Wayne Holder.

The program is divided into two parts. The first

part is called CLEANUP. This checks for punctuation errors, double words, capitalization errors, and makes sure that quotation marks, brackets, and other things that *should* come in pairs *do* come in pairs.

The second part is called PHRASE. PHRASE will find over 500 overused or frequently misused phrases, point them out, and suggest alternate (or correct) substitutions.

The idea behind dividing the program into two parts is that, once learned, the PHRASE part of the program will seldom need to be used. However, the errors in CLEANUP are often typos, and even the best grammarian may want to run his or her every letter through CLEANUP.

Both CLEANUP and PHRASE, unlike Grammatik, will mark the errors you want to change in the text. (With Grammatik you need a printed copy to mark changes on, then go back and find the changes in the text.)

On the whole, Punctuation and Style seems a more complete, sophisticated program than Grammatik, and at $125, it is highly recommended.

Keep in mind, however, that no program can check the grammar in a sentence that requires logical (ie: human) analysis. Nothing will replace a reading or two of *On Writing Well.* Even elaborate programs on mainframe computers designed to "improve" the written word can't be fully trusted.

One of these programs at the Bell Laboratories changed "Fourscore and seven years ago, our forefathers brought forth upon this continent a new nation, conceived in liberty and dedicated to the proposition that all men are created equal..." into "Eighty-seven years ago, our grandfathers created a free nation here."

Some things are best left to the word processor in the human mind.

Micro Link II

This is an easy to use, inexpensive communication package for almost any computer. It allows one computer to transfer information to and from another computer, or allows one computer to hook up to data bank services through a modem.

There are a great many communications programs around. I include this one because of its simplicity and price ($89).

SuperFile

SuperFile is a remarkable program that lets you file any information — from a word to a book — under as many as 250 different key words.

You can file a letter under not just who it was to or what it was about or the date written or who wrote the letter, but under all four — plus 246 other classifications. *Simultaneously.*

An address can be filed under not just last name, but first name, occupation, city, state, zip code, area code, likes, dislikes, where you met them, whether you ever want to meet them again, and 239 other vital statistics.

Quotes can be filed under who said them, when they were said, and 248 different subject categories.

Books, articles, photographs, music — anything you would not want to, or would not be able to, put into the computer — can be numbered, and that number filed under as many as 250 key words. For example, "Photo #1256" could be filed under the key words "waterfall, Canada, color, nature, 35mm," and hundreds more. Anytime you asked for photos of a waterfall, or scenes of Canada, or shots of nature, "Photo #1256" would be listed.

And now comes the best part. Not only does it file a bit of information in 250 categories simultaneously, it also allows you to combine key word requests. Only those bits of information that match *all* requested categories will appear.

If you were a classical music buff, Superfile could tell you how many hundred recordings of Beethoven's Fifth Symphony you had by simply asking for "BEETHO-VEN *and* FIFTH SYMPHONY." The several you might have by Toscanini could be found by typing in "BEETHO-VEN *and* FIFTH SYMPHONY *and* TOSCANINI."

You could ask SuperFile to search through your electronic address book and find all of your FRIENDS living in CLEVELAND who own a COMPUTER. Only those entries with the key words "friends," "computer," and "Cleveland" would be presented.

Further, a file can be created from a sorted list that allows you, using certain word processing programs, to add the information, automatically, into form letters. (WordStar is one of them. You can contact the SuperFile people for details on others.)

SuperFile is easy to use and, compared with other

data base management programs, inexpensive. ($195.) It carries an unprecedented 30-day money back guarantee. Use the program for 30 days. If you don't like it, send it back for a full refund. With the ease of copying a program disk and Xeroxing an instruction manual, it's nice to see a software company that actually *trusts* its customers.

The Random House Thesaurus

But don't lose any sleep over Grammatik's lost glory. The Grammatik people have now joined Dictronics, and Dictronics has come out with an excellent program that has, thus far, no competition. This is a beautiful (handsome, comely, seemly, attractive, lovely, pretty, fine) program. It is well thought out, intelligent (bright, clever, alert, discerning, shrewd, smart), yet simply presented.

I have not used a thesaurus five times in the past fifteen years, and yet I still find myself excited (ruffled, discomposed, perturbed, stimulated, agitated, eager, enthusiastic) about this program.

To use the Random House Thesaurus (Random House has no connection with the program, other than the money they make from their license to Dictronics) one places the cursor within the word that needs, uh, thesaurusizing, pushes the ESCAPE key twice, and within a second or two the top of the screen is filled with synonyms.

Select the synonym you want, move the cursor to that word, push the ESCAPE key again, and the program automatically replaces the original word with the newly selected word. If the original word was the best, the RETURN key returns you to the word processing program with nothing changed.

That it works as well and as effortlessly as it does covers the positive aspects of the word "excited" (stimulated, eager, enthusiastic.) The negative aspects of my excitement (ruffled, discomposed, perturbed, agitated) stem from the limitations of the program.

As I see them, the limitations are two. The first is that The Random House Thesaurus currently works only with WordStar and PeachText — fine for WordStar and

PeachText users, but what about the rest of the universe? (Soon to be released is a version that will work with any word processing program running on the IBM Personal Computer.)

The second limitation is that the full thesaurus takes 240K of disk capacity. Hence, to place a dictionary program *and* a thesaurus *and* a word processing program on one disk (assuming the second disk drive would be used for document files), would require a disk with more than 500K. And I remember when I thought 340K per drive was ostentatious.

The Dictronics folk are working on adapting The Random House Thesaurus to other word processing programs, and if I were them, I would have chosen WordStar and PeachText, too. They are, after all, the most popular and widely used word processing programs in the world.

There doesn't seem to be much way of getting around the disk capacity question. They fit a 60,000 word thesaurus into 240K, and that's pretty good. (They make special smaller versions — with less words, of course — in forms as small as 80K.) Those of us who want it all may have to bite the bullet and get large capacity drives, or even a hard disk.

In the mean time, I leave the thesaurus on the same disk as the word processing program, put my document files on another disk drive, and switch disks when it's time to spell-check. (The thesaurus is used throughout the editing process, the spell-check program less frequently.)

The Random House Thesaurus is $150.

PRINTERS

Epson

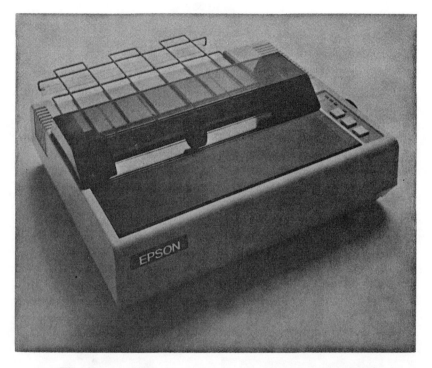

The Epson MX-80 is generally considered to be the best dot matrix printer in its price range ($500-$1,000). Of all the inexpensive dot matrix printers available, IBM chose the Epson as the printer for the IBM Personal Computer. The label says IBM, but the printer is Epson MX-80.

A dot matrix printer, for reasons detailed in the last chapter, should be considered for word processing only if the final appearance of printed copy need not look impressive.

Another reason for a dot matrix printer, particularly the MX-80, is that it travels well. Compact and weighing only twelve pounds, the MX-80 could be slipped into almost any suitcase. The MX-80 combined with one of the more portable computers listed below makes a great on-the-road word processor with full printing capabilities.

The MX-80 uses pins to feed continuous form paper. If you want to use letterhead stationery or single sheets of paper you'll need to buy the MX-80 FT.

SMITH-CORONA TP-1

The Smith-Corona TP-1 is made by one of the largest manufacturers of portable typewriters in the world. The TP-1 is Smith-Corona's first venture into the world of personal computer printers. Not surprisingly, the TP-1 resembles, in look and quality of construction, a portable electric typewriter with the keyboard removed.

The Smith-Corona TP-1 prints at the unspectacular speed of 12 characters per second. It does, however, use a daisy wheel (eleven type styles currently available) and prints sharp, uniform letter quality letters.

A letter on a 55 cps NEC Spinwriter might take a minute to print. That same letter on the TP-1 would take almost five. It is also not in the same league as the NEC in terms of rugged construction.

The TP-1 is, however, relatively inexpensive. It retails for $895, and is frequently discounted to somewhere between $600 and $700. In other words, it is a letter quality printer at a dot matrix price.

For the writer on a limited budget who needs to print only letters and occasional manuscripts, the TP-1 would be a good choice. For a business, or for a large-volume writer, the TP-1 might prove too slow. (The hourly cost of someone standing over a printer chugging away must be considered.)

It will be a year or more before the reliability of the TP-1 can be established. It is becoming very popular, so service should not be a problem.

Weighing only 18.5 pounds, the TP-1 would make an excellent traveling companion. (NEC Spinwriters weigh 45.5 pounds.)

If money is limited, and quality output is important, the TP-1 is the best choice.

Brother HR-1 (also Comrex CR-1)

The Brother HR-1 (also sold as the Comrex CR-1) is a bit faster than the Smith-Corona TP-1 (17 vs 12 characters per second), a bit quieter in operation, and, naturally, costs a bit more. ($1,150, although, like the Smith-Corona, it tends to be discounted.)

As of this writing, this is the least expensive letter-quality printer that will work with WordStar. (WordStar does not have a printer driver for the Smith-Corona, and Smith-Corona has not emulated any of the printers Word-Star supports.)

The Brother and the Comrex will do double strike, bold, and underline. They will not do proportional printing, super scripting or sub scripting.

Bytewriter

The Bytewriter is an Olivetti Praxis 30 electric type-writer with an interface that makes it a computer printer. It prints at about 10 characters per second. The cost is $795.

When not printing, the Bytewriter functions like the Olivetti Praxis typewriter it is.

If you need a typewriter *and* a printer *and* you're on a budget, this would be the printer to get.

Diablo and Qume

While Diablo and Qume both make fine printers, if you're going to spend that much money, my suggestion is to buy an NEC. This is based upon the superior reliability NECs over the years. The NEC is a workhorse.

If, however, you need a special feature offered by Diablo or Qume, or if you can get it for s special price, you will not be displeased with either printer.

Daisywriter

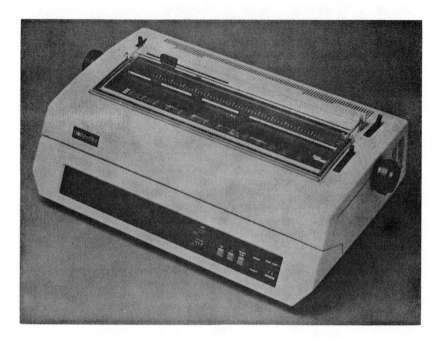

The Daisywriter is the least-expensive full-featured letter quality printer available. It will do true proportional printing, microspacing, superscripts, and subscripts. The Daisywriter retails for $1,495.

The Daisywriter features a 48K buffer, which allows you to enter the file to be printed into the *printer's* memory. While the printer is printing from its memory, your computer is free to be used for other tasks.

NEC

The NEC Spinwriter is a letter quality printer with an excellent reputation for print quality and durability. Time and time again I have heard unsolicited praise for the Spinwriter from people who know printers and have no vested interest in NEC or any other computer printer.

The Spinwriters print at a top speed of 55 characters per second, the fastest rated speed of any letter quality printer in its price range (around $3,000). A 35 CPS model is available that has all the Spinwriter features except speed, and this retails for about $2,500.

Printers and software are the most frequently discounted part of any personal computer system. Even if a dealer does not give discounts on the computer he or she will frequently take something off the printer. I see 55 CPS Spinwriters advertised for around $2,500 and 35 CPS Spinwriters for about $1,900.

All the above NEC prices include a device known as a tractor. A tractor pulls the paper through the printer by little pins on the left and right side of the page. This special perforated paper is known as **tractor paper** or **continuous form feed paper**. It's relatively endless so that page after page can be printed without stopping. It's good for rough drafts and for printing invoices, checks, and so forth.

Tractor paper is usually not of the best quality, but high-quality stationery can be glued or tipped onto standard tractor paper. This allows letter after letter to be printed without stopping to change paper after each sheet. This tipping process costs about $50 per thousand sheets and will work with envelopes, too. It's a good compromise between hand feeding and the expense of an automatic sheet feeder (about $1,500-$3,500).

If you don't mind feeding the sheets you print one at a time, rather like loading a standard typewriter, you can get the Spinwriter without the tractor and save about $200. If you're planning to use the printer for business applications right away, a tractor is recommended. If you might or might not use one eventually, the tractor can easily be added later.

A printer stand.

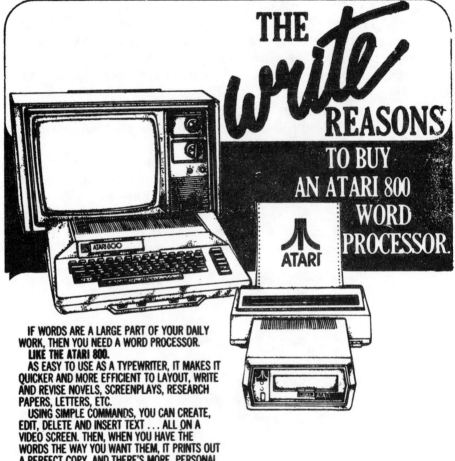

THE *write* REASONS
TO BUY AN ATARI 800 WORD PROCESSOR.

ATARI

IF WORDS ARE A LARGE PART OF YOUR DAILY WORK, THEN YOU NEED A WORD PROCESSOR. LIKE THE ATARI 800.

AS EASY TO USE AS A TYPEWRITER, IT MAKES IT QUICKER AND MORE EFFICIENT TO LAYOUT, WRITE AND REVISE NOVELS, SCREENPLAYS, RESEARCH PAPERS, LETTERS, ETC.

USING SIMPLE COMMANDS, YOU CAN CREATE, EDIT, DELETE AND INSERT TEXT . . . ALL ON A VIDEO SCREEN. THEN, WHEN YOU HAVE THE WORDS THE WAY YOU WANT THEM, IT PRINTS OUT A PERFECT COPY. AND THERE'S MORE. PERSONAL FINANCE, EDUCATION AND ENTERTAINMENT—ALL FOR UNDER $2800.00!

The write reasons, but the rong word processor

COMPUTERS

Apple, Atari, and Radio Shack TRS-80

Apple, Atari, and Radio Shack sell more personal computers than anyone else. Needless to say, their computers are very popular. Needless to say, their advertising campaigns are extensive and effective. Unfortunately, none of The Three Sisters makes a computer that adapts itself very well to word processing.

The thought of using an Atari for word processing is so absurd that at first I didn't even plan to include Atari in this review. Then I began reading computer ads in local newspapers. Guess which word processing system is advertised most often? You guessed it, Atari.

Atari makes a fine game-playing computer, one of the best, but when they start trying to turn their toy into a personal computer — especially a word processor — well, it makes about as much sense as suggesting that everyone ride bicycles to work.

The characters generated by Atari are fuzzy and hard to read, the power of the word processing programs limited, and the speed with which commands are executed is very slow. "All this for under $2,800!" the advertisement says. For under $2,800 you *can* buy a powerful word processing computer. It will not have the Atari name on it.

If you want to play games and do word processing buy a $150 Atari or a $250 Mattel Intellivision, attach it to your color TV, use that for games, then buy a personal computer from those discussed in this chapter and use that for word processing. Bicycles are wonderful, but chances are you'll want an automobile too.

The Apple and the Radio Shack TRS 80 each come in two models, Model II and Model III. The Apple II is the personal home computer, while the Apple III is the fancier version designed for business applications (or "Applecations," as the pun-hungry Apple people would say). The reverse is true of Radio Shack TRS-80s — Model III is the home computer while Model II is the business computer. (The Apple I and TRS-80 I have both been phased out.)

In both cases, the business computer is better suited to word processing. Unfortunately, the Apple III and TRS-80 II are not, in the current marketplace, good values. The money you would spend on either machine could buy more word processing power from other computers.

One of the major advantages of both Apple and Radio Shack is the vast array of programs that will run on them. With more computers in the field than anyone else, programmers naturally think first of Apple and Radio Shack. If you buy an Apple II or a TRS-80 III you will have a vast selection of programs that will run on your particular model and on none other. A program for an Apple II will not run on a TRS-80 III, and vice versa. Further, a program that will run on your Apple II will not even run on your Apple III! The same is true of Radio Shack: programs for the TRS-80 II and III are totally incompatible. The reasons for this are many, but behind them all is the familiar specter of corporate greed — there are high profits in software, and if someone buys a new computer it's nice to think that they will have to buy all new software as well.

Consequently, since the vast software selection designed for the home computer versions of Apple and Radio Shack will not run on the business versions of Apple and Radio Shack, the Apple III and the TRS-80 II must stand on their own merits and not on the plentiful software available for their less expensive siblings. The Apple III and TRS-80 II (as well as the newly introduced TRS-80 Model 16) are fine computers but, dollar for dollar, the competition has an edge on them.

This would leave one with the Apple II or the TRS-80 III. The owners of these two computers are legion and will swear by them. The Apple II, for example, plays wonderful, graphic games in full color — with sound effects. The TRS-80 III will lock your doors and turn off your lights at night and awaken you to the smell of freshly brewing coffee in the morning. None of this has very much to do with word processing, however.

The Apple II does not come with a video screen. When one is added, the screen display is made up of 24 lines which are but 40 characters in length. Word processing on a 40

An Apple II computer with two Apple Disk II drives and an Amdex video monitor

An Apple II keyboard

A TeleVideo 802 keyboard

character line is possible — thousands of people do it on Apples every day — but 80 character lines are far more comfortable. The keyboard on the Apple II is not detachable and has but 48 keys, compared with 80-or-so keys on other computers. (See photos.) The Apple keyboard lacks, among other things, a tab key, up and down cursor keys and a numeric keypad. (I talked with an accountant who purchased an Apple on which he planned to write his financial statements. With neither a numeric keypad nor a tab key — necessary for moving from one column to another — he couldn't have made a poorer choice.)

An Apple II can be tortured into a decent word processor — at great expense. All additions to Apples are made through rather expensive plug-in circuit boards known as "cards." You could add a card that would increase the line display from 40 to 80 characters; you would lose some clarity of display, but you would have an 80-character line. Then you could add a Z-80 card, then a CP/M card and, while you were at it, you would no doubt want to increase the memory with a memory card. Two disk drives would have to be added, which requires a disk controller card. It gets to be complicated and expensive, rather like buying a Chevrolet and, by adding every luxury option in the book, trying to turn it into a Cadillac. A Cadillac would not only have been cheaper, but it would have been a Cadillac.

The TRS-80 III is a bit better suited to word processing. It has a numeric keypad, tab, and cursor movement keys. The keyboard has a cheap feel, but it is adequate. The keyboard is not detachable.

The major drawback of the TRS-80 III is the built-in video display. The lines are 64 characters long, which is acceptable, but there are only 16 of them on the screen. Beyond that, the clarity and sharpness of the characters are among the worst I have seen on any full-size personal computer. (Not as bad as Atari, but still bad.)

This may sound as though I have a personal vendetta against Apple, Atari, and Radio Shack. I do not. They make fine computers that do many tasks well, word processing not being one of them. People who do word processing on Apples, Ataris, and TRS-80s will no doubt tell you they are wonderful, and they are — when compared with the electric typewriters those people were using before.

It's unfortunate that I cannot recommend these three computers more highly. There is hardly a town in America that does not have a Radio Shack store, and hardly a computer store in America that does not carry Apple and/or Atari. The support these three computers have is phenomenal, and there's nothing like support when a simple question needs answering right in the middle of The Great American Book Report.

I sincerely hope that as time goes on and this book is updated I will be able to recommend an Apple or an Atari or a Radio Shack word processing computer with unbridled enthusiasm.

(Note to Apple II users: If you plan to add word processing software to your Apple, you might want to look into Supertext by MUSE software. You won't need to add quite as many cards as you would for WordStar, and if you don't need all the features of WordStar, Supertext could save you some money.)

Franklin ACE 1000

The Franklin ACE 1000 keyboard includes a 12-key numeric pad, an alpha lock key and keys with special VisiCalc designations.

If for some reason you feel you *must* buy an Apple II for word processing, you might want to investigate the Franklin ACE 1000. The basic ACE 1000 costs about the same as the basic Apple II, but includes a better keyboard (although, like the Apple, it is not detachable), a numeric keypad, and 64K of RAM. All of the plug-in cards, programs, and peripherals made for the Apple will work with the Franklin ACE.

The ACE is better suited to word processing than the Apple II (you can get almost every peripheral for the Apple but a new keyboard). The ACE, however, requires the plug-in card for 80-columns (like the Apple II, the standard is 40). The ACE requires a plug-in card for color.

The ACE is in fact so close to the Apple II that Apple is suing ACE. (Apple seems to be suing *everyone* these days. Why don't they come out with a line of great new computers and let everyone else imitate their dust? As it stands they're trying to get universal proprietary rights on 1977 technology. Why?)

I don't think the ACE 1000 is a great value in computers if all you want to do is word processing. However, if for some reason you feel you *must* buy an Apple II for word processing...

Commodore

Commodore makes an amazing — if not confusing — array of computers. Try as I might, I have not been able to find one that I can recommend as a word processor.

The VIC-20 is a great value in small, introductory computers. (At $300 it's a much better buy than Radio Shack's Color Computer and, for many, better than the Atari 400 or 800.) But the 22 character lines, the fact that the screen display is not terribly sharp, the fact that there is not powerful word processing software available, etc. etc. would put it in the Atari category of word processing.

The PET has only 40 characters per line, hence the drawbacks of the Apple apply.

The 8032, or CBM — Commodore Business Machine — is best suited to word processing. The problem is that it is not a CP/M based machine and therefore one is locked into the Commodore software. At the present this does not include a spell-check program. Further, the keyboard is not detachable.

The Commodore 64 is a CP/M machine, but, again, has only 40 characters per line. Sigh.

Commodore seems to be after the Apple/Atari market

at the moment. Their computers, advertising and pricing reflect this, and they seem to be doing a good job of it. When they decide to go after the IBM/Xerox market, then Commodore will be in the word processing business.

"Gentlemen, Mr. Spock's replacement has arrived."

Heath/Zenith

The Heath H-89 is not the greatest personal computer in the world, but it's not bad. For word processing, it is better than the Apple II or TRS-80 III or Atari in almost all ways. The screen display is a full 24 eighty-character lines. It has not one but two Z-80 microprocessors. It is CP/M based. It has an 80 character keyboard with a numeric keypad. It offers both WordStar and PeachText, available directly from Heath. Not bad.

The drawbacks of the Heath H-89 with regard to word processing are: The keyboard is not detachable. The video display is not the world's sharpest. It has but one disk drive although more can be added.

The H-89 has one advantage that no other full-size personal computer offers: It comes in a kit form and you put it together yourself. This may not seem like much of an advantage, but putting together one's personal computer personally can be surprisingly enjoyable. (Assembled, the H-89 is distributed by Zenith as the Z-89. The H-89 sells for $1,895, the Z-89 for $2,895.)

I would think that the H-89 would be a fine word processor for someone who wanted to learn about computers from the inside out on a limited budget.

The Osborne 1

The Osborne 1 is a funny computer, as fascinating and idiosyncratic as the man who designed it, Adam Osborne. Adam Osborne wrote about computers until he finally decided he could do a better job of computer manufacturing than the companies he was writing about, so he formed Osborne Computer Company and the rest is recent history.

The main advantages of the Osborne 1 are price and portability.

For $1,795 you get a computer with 64K of RAM, video display, two disk drives (92K capacity per drive), a semidetachable keyboard with numeric keypad, a Z-80 microprocessor and enough programs to open your own software store. You get CP/M, WordStar, MailMerge, SuperCalc (an electronic spreadsheet program), and not one but two BASIC programs, MBASIC (Microsoft Basic) and CBASIC.

All this fits into a 23.5-pound package that is portable — not portable like a calculator is portable, but portable like a portable sewing machine is portable. Portable or not, in the world of personal computers, it is an unbelievable value.

The keyboard is good. It has a numeric keypad, ten programmable function keys and separate cursor movement keys that work with WordStar.

The Osborne 1, alas, has a tragic flaw. It can be summed up in three words: The Video Display. The built-in video screen has a diagonal measurement that is slightly smaller than five inches.

The screen displays 24 lines of text, but each line is only 52 characters long. This is barely acceptable for word processing. An external video monitor enlarges the size of the screen to a "regulation" twelve inches, but the 52-character line length remains. When blown up on the larger video screen, the characters are readable but not too sharp.

A company known as JMM Enterprises sells various peripheral adapters for the Osborne 1. One I would certainly recommend is the four-foot keyboard extension cable. This makes the keyboard truly detachable. Another from JMM is Mondapt, which stands for Monitor Adaptor. This allows you to attach any video monitor to the Osborne 1. (The

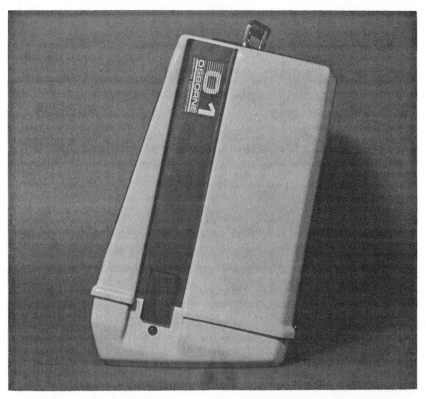

Folded, the Osborne 1 resembles a tipsy sewing machine

The new version of the Osborne 1, unfolded

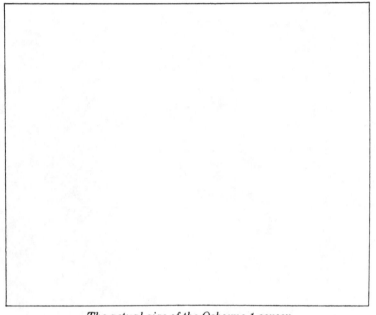

The actual size of the Osborne 1 screen

Osborne 1 normally allows only the attachment of their own not very spectacular, rather expensive $250 monitor.) The Mondapt II from JMM allows the Osborne 1 to use an ordinary TV as a video display with results that teeter on the brink of total unacceptability.

KAYPRO II (Formerly KAYCOMP II)

My review of the Osborne 1 in *Popular Computing* included the following:

It's easy to speculate on how the Osborne 1 *might* have been designed to hold a larger screen. First, the various input/output ports could have been placed at the rear of the machine...This would have removed the ports from the front panel, where they are generally a nuisance. With a modem, a printer, an IEEE-488 peripheral, and the keyboard all attached to the computer by means of wide, flat cable, approaching the disk

drive is almost as difficult as mating with a reluctant octopus.

Next, the disks could have been mounted horizontally and placed beside each other, leaving room for a 7-or 8-inch video monitor.

Well, the KayPro people moved the input/output ports to the rear, mounted their drives not horizontally but vertically, and made room for not a 7-or 8-inch but a *nine*-inch monitor. This allows for a full 24 lines with 80 characters per line. The screen is green phosphor. (The Osborne is black & white.)

The screen is more readable than the Osborne, even with the Osborne 12-inch video monitor attached.

The keyboard of the KayPro II is excellent. It has a detachable keyboard with six feet of coiled cable. The KayPro II weighs about two pounds more than the Osborne 1.

The two built-in disk drives each hold 191K of information (compared with Osborne's 92). 64K of memory is standard (same as Osborne).

The case is metal, as opposed to Osborne's molded plastic. (The new Osborne case looks more sophisticated, although the KayPro II has an attractive "high tech" look. When standing on end the KayPro II is not tipsy. Certainly metal is more rugged than plastic.)

Put simply, the KayPro II is — in terms of hardware — equal to or better than one of the greatest computer success stories of modern times, the Osborne 1. Its cost? The same as the Osborne 1, $1,795. (What a coincidence, hey?)

The KayPro II, like the Osborne 1, offers a small software store free with purchase. CP/M, SBASIC, Profit Plan (an electronic spreadsheet), and the entire line of Perfect software. ("Perfect" is a trade name, not necessarily a product description.) This includes Perfect Writer (reviewed earlier), Perfect Filer, Perfect Calc (yet another electronic spreadsheet), and Perfect Speller.

The weak link in the Perfect chain is Perfect Speller. It checks for root words and then adds prefixes and suffixes to them. This means that not-real words, made up of acceptable prefixes, acceptable suffixes, and acceptable root words, could slip by. "Thoughful" for "thoughtful," "verbage" for "verbiage," or "courtious" for "courteous," might not be tagged for correction. Given the state-of-the-art of spell check programs, this is unacceptable. For spell checking, buy The Word Plus.

This weak link in no way detracts from the value of the KayPro II or its generous offering of software. Osborne doesn't give away any type of spell check program — good, bad, or otherwise.

I am pleased with the way the KayPro people respond to the comments of the marketplace. Criticized by some for the word processing program they once offered (Select), KayPro offered another (Perfect Writer). I am pleased, too, with the support the Kaypro people are giving those who have already purchased the Kaypro II. For only $75, current owners of the KayPro II can add the entire collection of Perfect software to their machines. (A retail value of almost $1,000!)

But that's not all. For the home they include three

programs: Family Budget, Net Worth Statement, and Income Tax.

For a small business they include Income Statement, Cost of Goods, Expense Reports, Accounts Receivable, Accounts Payable, Invoice Entry, Cash Flow Assessment, and Payroll Analysis.

But wait! There's more! For the investor there are a series of programs to analyze stocks, real estate, professional fees, break even, and CHI-Squares. (Don't ask me what a CHI-Square is. All I know is that you can analyze one with a KayPro II.)

This is certainly the most impressive array of free-with-purchase software included with any machine at any price.

Yes, the economical computer of choice is the KayPro II. Matched with the Smith-Corona TP-1, it gives you a great word processor for less than $2,500.

Some computers are more portable than others.

Otrona Attache

The Otrona Attache is a portable personal computer that begins to approach true portability. It weighs eighteen pounds — five pounds less than the Osborne. The Attache is also smaller and more compact.

The screen size of the Attache is the same five inches as the Osborne, but the display is a full 24 eighty-character lines. Because the Otrona uses a high-resolution screen, each character is sharper than on the Osborne. Further, the screen is capable of high-quality graphics, something the Osborne is not.

Two 5¼-inch disk drives are built in, each drive holding 380K of storage, more than four times the Osborne's capacity.

And the price for all these wonders? You guessed it, more than twice as much as the Osborne, $3,995. That price includes CP/M, WordStar, Microsoft Basic, and a graphics package. It does not include MailMerge, CBASIC, or Super-Calc, which the Osborne does.

The Attache keyboard is truly detachable. It uses standard coiled telephone cable (the kind that goes between the handset and the phone), so a 25-foot extension cable can be purchased at your local Phone Store for $9.95. The keyboard is full-size and responsive. The numeric keypad has been omitted due to space limitations, a wise choice.

The cursor keys move the cursor around in WordStar, and the keyboard has several of the most commonly used WordStar commands assigned to clearly labeled keys on the top row. This would allow one not familiar with WordStar to perform basic editing functions with very little training.

For larger screen display the Otrona will plug into any video monitor.

Escort

A few years ago I started a publishing company. I called it Lion Press because lions were my favorite animals and I had a mane of hair that made me look like a character out of *The Wizard of Oz*.

I commissioned my favorite cartoonist, Charles Addams, to draw the colophon (trademark). I asked him to revise a *New Yorker* cover he had drawn in which a lion was pointing to a chart depicting the hierarchy of the animal kingdom with, naturally, the lion at the top.

I requested that, rather than ordinary animals, the chart include the colophons — especially the animal colophons — of all the other publishers: Bantam's rooster, Penguin's penguin, Pocket Book's kangaroo, Knopf's dog — even Simon & Schuster's human.

Proudly I took out ads in *Publishers Weekly* announcing my new company and our Charles Addams colophon. Stationery was printed, business cards, envelopes, and 20,000 copies of our first book. Like falling in love, it was expensive, but worth it.

Then one day I came home to find a message on my service: Mr. Ross from Lion Books had called. From Lion Books? But *I* was Lion Books; Lion Press, actually, but it was the same thing.

I called Mr. Ross, who kindly explained to me that

12/31/75

he too thought there was little difference between Lion Books and Lion Press. He, however, had started Lion Books ten years before.

We agreed that there was only room in the publishing jungle for one Lion. I asked him if he would like a good buy on a colophon and some beautiful stationery.

I empathize, then, with Jonos Ltd., makers of the Courier Portable Computer. After ads and circulars and operating manuals and stationery, ITT contacted Jonos and let them know that ITT was already making a computer product, a terminal, known as the Courier.

Jonas decided that one might be able to fight City Hall, but not ITT. (The ITT person who contacted them had the title "Senior Staff Trademark Counsel." How would you like to fight a trademark infringement case against a company that had a Senior Staff Trademark Counsel?)

Jonos renamed their computer. It's now called the Escort.

The Escort combines the portability of the Attache with the large (9-inch) screen of the KayPro II. It does this by using the Sony 3½-inch MicroFloppy disk drives. These take up less room (and have less weight) than 5¼-inch drives. Two are built into the Escort (with a generous 322K per drive).

The Escort costs the same as the Otrona, $3,995. That price includes CP/M, Spellbinder (word processing), Spellguard (spell checking) Multiplan (electronic worksheet), and Microsoft BASIC.

If it's portability you're after, be sure to compare the Otrona Attache with the Escort and see which one you prefer.

In the meanwhile, the Escort people spend each day hoping the Senior Staff Trademark Counsel from Ford Motor Company does not get in touch, just as we at Prelude Press fear that long-overdue call from Honda.

Sony Typecorder

While on the subject of portability, I thought I would mention the Sony Typecorder. The Typecorder is not a personal computer. It will not run programs. It has no video screen or disk drives. It is, however a highly portable word recorder.

The name Typecorder is descriptive. It has a tape recorder that will record dictation on a microcassette. It also has a typewriter keyboard that will record words on the same microcassette. The whole thing is the size of an 8½ x 11 sheet of paper, is 1½ inches thick and weighs three pounds. It costs $1,500.

Words are typed into the standard QWERTY keyboard and displayed on a single-line, forty-character liquid crystal display, the same sort of display most hand-held calculators currently use. Forty characters is about half a line, and after a full line a carriage return must be hit. (No word wrap on the Typecorder.) About 50 pages of text can be stored on the microcassette. The microcassette can then be turned over for the storage of another fifty.

You can scroll forward or backward in the text, making changes as you go. As you can imagine, having one-half line displayed at any one time severely limits editing. The battery lasts more than five hours, long enough for a cross-country flight.

The text can then be transferred to your personal computer through an optional communication package. Here it can be edited using whatever word processing software you have. The microcassette can also fit directly into the Sony word processor, a stand alone word processor that is nice but, at $10,000, a bit expensive. If you have unlimited funds, however...

The Typecorder itself, at $1,500, is also expensive. If you are addicted to recording your words through a keyboard, as I seem to be, and if you spend a great deal of time on airplanes or commuter trains or in the High Sierras backpacking, the Sony Typecorder might prove an excellent addition to whichever word processing computer you select.

Epson HX-20

In the world of truly portable word recorders, one must certainly include the Epson HX-20. The Epson includes a full keyboard (better than the Typecorder), a 20-character four-line screen, and a built-in 20-column dot matrix printer. The price is $895. A microcassette can be added for around $200. The batteries of the HX-20 last a remarkable 50 hours. Recharging time is 8 hours.

As of this writing, there is no method for storing words on the HX-20, although a program for doing that is promised by February, 1982. When that is available, the Epson HX-20 will be an invaluable "peripheral" for frequently traveling writers.

The Teleram T-3000

Where do companies get their numbers from? I mean, what connection does the number "3000" have with this computer? I can't figure it out. I imagine a group of Vice Presidents in Charge of Product Naming were sitting around one day, and one said, "What shall we call this thing?"

Another said, "How about the Teleram 1?"

"No," another said, "Osborne already has the Osborne 1."

"Well, how about the Teleram II? It has a nice alliterative quality."

"I don't think so. There's already a KayPro II, and a *Superman II*, and *Tea for Two*."

"Teleram III?"

"Apple III, *Three's Company*..."

"Let's tie it to the machine somehow. What does it weigh?"

"About nine pounds."

"How about the Teleram Nine?"

"No. Ice-Nine, *Plan Nine from Outer Space*. Besides, *nein* is 'no' in German. 'Teleram' is a German Sounding name, like Telefunken. We don't want anyone to think the Germans said 'no' to this product.

"Well, what does the thing cost?"

"Oh, around $3,000."

"That's it! The Teleram 3000!"

A quick check of all known products, movies, television shows, and song titles revealed that nothing had ever been named 3000 before.

"It's good. It's very good," said the head of the Product Naming Division, who up until this time had been silent. "But we need a zinger, a grabber...an alliteration, a rhyme..." He drew deep within himself, lost for a moment in creative thought.

The room was so still you could hear a microchip counting.

The head of the Product Naming Division returned from his reverie. "The Teleram T-3000," he announced.

"Brilliant, J.B.!"

"Superb!"

"Incredible!"

"It has alliteration. It has rhyme. You're a genius, J.B."

J.B. looked at the floor and shuffled his feet. "I just do my job the best I can," he said, and the Teleram T-3000 was born.

I don't mean to pick on Teleram. The same is true of almost any numbered computer (or any numbered consumer product): What on earth do those numbers have to do with reality? Who makes them up? Do they get paid? Does it add a nickel to the cost of everything we buy? I wish Ralph Nader would investigate this one.

The Teleram T-3000 (hereinafter referred to as the Teleram) is the most portable full-function computer available. It's perfect for people who travel a lot on planes or commuter trains. (I assume anyone who can afford that many plane tickets or a house in the country can afford a $2,995 computer.)

The Teleram weighs about nine pounds, has a full-function keyboard, and four eighty-character lines of display. The display is liquid crystal, like pocket calculators. While one would not want to write a magnum opus on a four line screen, it's surprisingly useable — far more so than the one-half line displays found in other portables.

The Teleram stores information on a bubble memory. Bubble memory is user-changeable, like RAM, but it keeps the information indefinitely, even when the power is turned off, like ROM. It's a great combination of the two, but, at the moment, fairly expensive. The $2,995 price includes 128K of bubble memory. An additional 128K is $600.

128K is usually more than sufficient. A word processing program might take half of it (Wordstar, for example, consumes 68K), which would leave about 60K (30 double-spaced typewritten pages) for files. After a journey, the document files would be transferred to disks, and the memory erased, leaving 60K again for the next trip.

The batteries of the Teleram last about five hours before recharging. In the near future, an interface unit, disk drives, and a video monitor will be available. This would allow the Teleram to be used as a regular computer in the home or office, and a portable computer on the road.

The Teleram will also plug into any computer, and data can be transferred to or from the Teleram.

Teleram is best known for its portable workstations used by journalists throughout the country. If they can build reliable terminals that hold up to the daily grind of on-the-road reporters, you can bet they have the technology to make a reliable portable computer.

Morrow Micro Decision

This is a fine computer and an excellent value. In terms of overall value it runs neck and neck with the KayPro II. The Morrow has a larger screen than the Kay-Pro II, but it costs a bit more and it's not portable.

The standard Morrow Micro Decision computer comes with one disk drive (186K formatted capacity); a 12-inch green phosphor screen (25 80-character lines); a Z80A processor; 64K of RAM; a detachable keyboard with a numeric keypad, separate cursor movement keys, and seven programmable function keys.

And that's not all: Morrow is a member-in-good-standing of the Great Software Giveaway Program. You

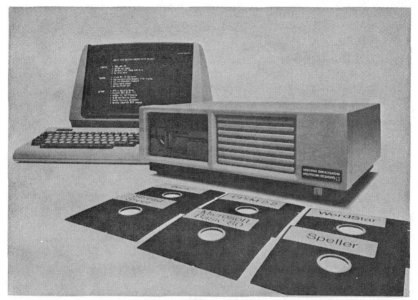

get, free with purchase, CP/M, Pilot (a program that makes CP/M more friendly), WordStar, Microsoft BASIC (MBASIC), BaZic (for NorthStar compatibility), Correct-It (a spell-check program), and LogiCalc (an electronic spreadsheet).

All this for $1,790. One more 186K disk drive (highly recommended) brings the price to $2,140.

The screen display is sharp, clear, and legible. (On the prototype monitor I saw, the lines undulated ever so slightly. I'm hoping this will be corrected in production units.) The keyboard is solid, with a good feel. My only complaint, as a user, is the noise the disk drives make. Sometimes they sound like a subway braking, and at other times they sound like Darth Vadar breathing. I'm hoping that (A) the noises were only in the drives I listened to, or (B) not everyone is as delicate about the sound of disk drives as I am.

I first heard about the Morrow Micro Decision the way I hear about most things these days: a letter from a reader. This reader wrote:

"The company is MORROW DESIGNS out of San Leandro (California) and seems to be a well established producer of hard disks and S-100 type board components.

DUN'S Directory tells me they have thirty-five employees and the listed officers are all named Morrow. I have traced their ads back to 1979."

I do believe I have the most wonderful readers in the world. I wrote back and told him he should consider working for *Sixty Minutes*.

I do not know how many employees Morrow has (I do know the boss is named Mr. Morrow), but I know they have a good reputation and have been around the computer world longer than I have. They are a solid company, and will no doubt stand behind their product.

However, it is a new computer, and the precautions that apply to any new computer do apply. As Fats Waller said more than once, "One never knows, do one?"

The Morrow Micro Decision is a great computer at a great price, and well worth your consideration.

Sanyo MBC 1000

The Sanyo is also a great computer at a great price. It is similar to the Morrow, except whereas Morrow gives extra software, Sanyo gives extra disk capacity. (186K per drive on the Morrow, 326K per drive on the Sanyo.)

The basic Sanyo includes one disk drive (326K); a 12-inch green phosphor screen (25 80-character lines); 64K of RAM; and adetachable keyboard with separate cursor movement keys, numeric keypad, and five function keys. Also included is CP/M and SBASICII.

The price is $1,795. An additional disk drive is $395. (The extra disk sits in its own cabinet off to one side.) This would bring the price of a two-drive system to $2,190. All you'd have to add is a word processing program and a printer.

The weak link of the Sanyo is the screen display. The characters are formed using only a 6x7 dot resolution, and the dots are therefore noticeable. The display, however, is far from intolerable, and better than, say, Apple II or Radio Shack III. (But not as good as Morrow.)

The Sanyo is likely to be sold in a bundled package — computer, printer, software, everything — for one price.

For example, I saw the Sanyo in Los Angeles at a place called The Support Group. They sell the Sanyo (single disk), WordStar, and a Comrex printer for $2,995.

The Sanyo MBC 1000 is the least expensive, high disk capacity computer on the market.

Cromemco

Configured for word processing, the Cromemco offers a keyboard, monochrome (green) video screen, Z80 processor, 64K of memory, two 390K 5¼-inch disk drives, a "CP/M-compatible" operating system, a word processing program, a spreadsheet program, and a structured BASIC program. All this will cost you $2,380.

If you'd like to economize, you can leave off one of the disk drives, and the entire package would cost $1,785. A second disk drive can be added later for $595.

The keyboard, although detachable, is small and does not include a numeric keypad. The programs are Cromemco's Own. I have not had a chance to use them, so I cannot comment on them. Since they come free with a

computer that is a a good buy even without software, if the software doesn't meet your needs, you can always buy a program that does.

Although this is a new computer, Cromemco has been making small computers for some time. Let's hope the bugs that so often plague new computers have been worked out in design and testing, and not in the marketplace. (This hope, disclaimer, and warning are true of *all* newly introduced computers.)

This is a good, economical, and welcome addition to the world of personal computing.

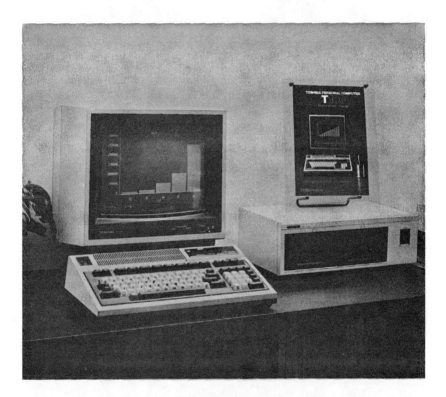

Toshiba T100

A Toshiba personal computer, configured for word processing, would include a full-function keyboard, a monochrome (green) screen, Z80 processor, 64K of memory, two 280K 5¼-inch disk drives, and CP/M. All this for $2,480.

The weak link in this system is the video display. Although an 8x8 dot-matrix character generation should be adequate, for some reason the letters look broken and spotty. This could just be the display of the unit I saw, or it might be inherent in the design. I would recommend comparing the video display quality with other comparably priced personal computers before you buy.

A positive aspect of the video display is that, with the simple addition of a color monitor, the T100 is capable of full-color graphic display.

The Eagle II

There is lots of good news and one piece of bad news about the Eagle II computer. First the good news:

It has a good keyboard, fine screen, Z80 processor, 64K of memory, two 360K 5¼-inch disk drives, and costs but $2,995. More good news: The $2,995 price also includes CP/M, CBASIC, UltraCalc spreadsheet, and the Spellbinder word processing program.

A great buy, that. And now for the bad news: It does not have a detachable keyboard. To quote Charlie Brown, "Arghhhh!"

A detachable keyboard? I'll give you a detachable keyboard.

NorthStar Advantage

NorthStar has been making computers for a number of years, their Horizon being one of the most respected and dependable ever made. The Advantage is NorthStar's first "all-in-one" computer. (The Horizon requires the addition of a terminal.) They have made a fine machine, reasonably priced (around $4,000). Unfortunately they took the concept of all-in-one a bit too far: The keyboard is not detachable. For reasons detailed in the last chapter, a nondetachable keyboard is a major drawback in word processing applications.

The Advantage has one advantage: It does high-quality computer graphics. Any business that needs graphics *and* word processing would do well to consider the Advantage.

TeleVideo 802

TeleVideo is one of the foremost manufacturers of inexpensive, high quality video terminals. In 1981 they introduced several personal and business computers, and the 802 is the latest addition to that line.

It's a fine computer and a good value. They took their popular top-of-the-line 950 terminal and added 64K of memory, a Z-80 processor and two disk drives with 340K per drive. With a CP/M operating system included, the retail price is $3,495. Discounts are frequently available.

The keyboard is detachable, and the screen display is one of the best. There are 24 eighty-character lines, numeric keypad, cursor movement keys, and 22 programmable function keys. The keyboard and screen are state-of-the-art all the way.

The major problem with the TeleVideo 802 is that it is not distributed as widely as some of the other computers discussed in this section. Therefore, finding a neighborhood store with 802 experts might be difficult. Let's hope this situation improves over time.

Xerox 820-II

The Xerox 820-II is the revised version of the Xerox 820. It has a detachable keyboard with numeric keypad and separate cursor keys, black and white video display (24 80-character lines), 64K of RAM, and a Z80A processor. This basic unit costs $2,245.

Disk drives can them be added in 5¼-inch, 8-inch, and hard disk formats. Two 5¼-inch drives, with 360K of storage per drive, run $1,450. CP/M is an additional $200.

This would put the price of a Xerox 820-II, configured like a TeleVideo 802, to $3,895.

Sales abound, however, in the Land of Xerox. Contact your local Xerox Store for the latest special.

Hewlett Packard HP 86 and HP 125

Hewlett Packard is one of the big names in the computer business. They cater to business, and this is reflected by their computers — and by their prices.

The top of the line "personal" computer is the HP 125. It has a good screen, good keyboard, two 5¼-inch drives (270K per drive), 64K of memory, a Z80 processor, and CP/M. As a personal computer to be used as a word processor, it meets all criteria except value: it's almost $5,000.

The HP 125 is not sold as a personal computer, however. It's official designation is "HP 125 Business Assistant." While $5,000 is too much to pay for a personal computer, $5,000 for a Business Assistant is *cheap.*

The personal personal computer is the HP 86. It seems more patched together than designed. The basic unit (keyboard, memory, and processor) is $1,795. 260K 5¼-inch disk drives are $850 *each*. And a monitor is $325. It is not a CP/M based machine, although I was told a plug-in module was available for an undisclosed amount.

This adds up to a machine with the appearance and capabilities of a Toshiba, but the price of a IBM.

When I voiced my concern about prices to the HP salespeople, I was told that these were only the retail

The HP 125

prices, and that dealers frequently sold the machines for much less.

That being the case, I would say that the HP 125 would make a good Word Processing Assistant if sold for $3,500 to $4,000.

The HP 86 would have to sell for about $2,500 — including the CP/M module — before it could successfully compete.

NEC APC

NEC, the people who make the finest letter-quality printer around, make several small computers marketed by at least two different divisions.

The one that seems to be getting the most attention is the APC, which stands for Advanced Personal Computer. As fond as I am of the NEC printers, I must admit I am not very fond of the APC.

The keyboard is solid, and the screen display is clear, but then so is the keyboard and screen display of computers costing half as much. The drives are 8-inch, and only 8-inch. They are also the noisiest drives I have heard on a small computer.

The processor is 16-bit. The software for the APC is limited, and there is no adapter card for running 8-bit software.

All this for $3,998. If it were $2,000 cheaper, it might be a breakthrough. As it is, it's not a great word processing value.

The strength of this machine seems to be when a color monitor is added. This is of little importance to a word processing computer, although a business that requires color graphics would appreciate the sharpness of the color display. (And if you're someone who *must* do word processing in color, this would be a machine to investigate.) (The color monitor adds about $1,000 to the price.)

At various points in this book when I recommend buying an NEC, please keep in mind that I am referring to the *Spinwriter Letter Quality Printer*, and not the Advanced Personal Computer.

Alas.

The Lanier TypeMaster

I know I said I wouldn't review stand alone word processors, but I think it's time for a little comic relief, brought to us by the people who brought us No Problem Typing: Lanier.

Before I tell you the amazing price, let me tell you what you get. You get a keyboard and a screen. So far so good. You get two disk drives with a whopping 70K per drive. You get software and a year's service contract.

And you get a printer — *built in.*

Yes, your paper goes in the top of the TypeMaster not unlike bread in a toaster. *I am not making this up.* There is really a printer built into this word processor. All-in-one has never been — and pray Heaven never again will be — taken this far.

The price for this desktop marvel? "We're having a Special this month. It's only around $9,000." The voice behind the Special Price was the Lanier salesperson, one of those salespeople who you don't just want to have an affair with: You want to get *married* and raise a *family.*

So, if you're tired of singles bars, in need of a good chuckle, have money to burn and bread to toast, visit your local Lanier office. Or just given them a call: they'll come to *you.*

(Be sure to ask about the TypeMaster with the built-in dishwasher, bottle opener, coffee maker, and pasta machine. It's on Special next month.)

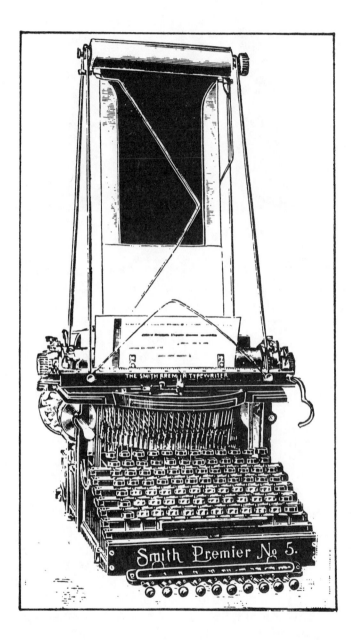

IBM Personal Computer

I have said more than a few disparaging words about IBM in this book, but truth be told, when it came time to make a personal computer, they did it right. It has been out about a year and already it is the standard by which all other personal computers are measured.

The keyboard is excellent. The touch is firm and sure. It's detachable, although heavier than most detachable keyboards. As good as it is, the keyboard has two drawbacks. First, the shift key is the size of a regular key, which is far smaller than shift keys usually are. This is compounded by the fact that just below the shift key is a larger key labeled ALT (for Alternate.) It's very easy to hit the ALT, or any other key surrounding the shift key, because of the shift key's smaller size. Further still, the shift key is not located directly next to the Z key, as is the standard, so one often hits the backslash key (which is located next to the Z) rather than the shift key. (Why the inventors of the industry standard "Selectric Keyboard" didn't follow their own standard is beyond me.)

Second, the cursor movement keys are located on the numeric keypad. This means that you can either use the cursor keys *or* you can use the numeric keypad. A special shift key must be depressed to change from one mode to the other. This could prove inconvenient in typing financial statements or documents containing many numbers.

There is an audible and tactile "click" each time a key is depressed on the keyboard. It is subtle, rather like turning a small electrical switch on and off (which, in fact, is exactly what you're doing). Some people find this verification of a keystroke that can be both heard and felt delightful, others find it irritating. You'll have to decide if you fall into the "some" camp or the "others" camp. The keyboard on the IBM personal computer is unlike any other.

The screen is sharp and easy to read. It displays 24 lines, eighty characters per line. The monochrome screen is green phosphor. Graphics are fully supported on the IBM.

The IBM is sold in modular units that allow you to build a system to your liking. A 64K system with two 5¼-inch disk drives (340K per drive), keyboard, and video display would cost around $4,000. (It is doubtful that you will find or receive a discount on an IBM, but it can't hurt to try.)

The IBM personal computer is pioneering the use of a 16-bit microprocessor. (Until the IBM, all personal computers used an 8-bit microprocessor.) Sixteen-bit microprocessors promise faster and more powerful computing in the future, although the power and speed will affect numerical computing far more than it will word processing.

Unfortunately, the 16-bit microprocessor will not run currently available software, CP/M or any other, without major rewriting. Most software houses are stumbling all over each other to make these changes and to market "IBM Compatible" programs. As of this writing, however, the IBM software pickings are slim. (WordStar and EasyWriter II are available.)

Until the many CP/M programs are adapted for the IBM, Lifeboat Associates is marketing an emulator that will permit standard 8-bit software to run on the 16-bit IBM. It's called the EM-80. It slows down the operating speed of the word processing program, but is a good stop-gap until the modified 16-bit software hits the market.

Another solution (in many ways a better one) is known as the Baby Blue Card. (IBM is known in computer

circles as Big Blue after, I suppose, the big blue letters that make up its trademark.) This is a card that plugs into the IBM Personal Computer and allows it to run all existent 8-bit CP/M software. It also adds 64K to the memory. It costs $600. This would give one an eight *and* a sixteen-bit machine.

Eight-bit personal computers have a de facto standard operating system, CP/M. Sixteen-bit computers are still battling it out. The two leading contenders are CP/M-86, a version of CP/M for 16-bit machines, and MS-DOS — also known as IBM-DOS. As I'm sure you have guessed by now, a program written for CP/M-86 will not run on MS-DOS and vice versa. Until the marketplace decides the 16-bit personal computer operating system standard, confusion and incompatibility will reign.

Once again, Lifeboat comes to the rescue. For a mere $75 they sell CP/EMULATOR (CP/M-ulator — get it?). This operating system will run programs written in either CP/M-86 or MS-DOS. Although this program has certain limitations, it is recommended for anyone considering the IBM personal computer. As time goes on, the IBM is likely to be the best-supported personal computer on the market.

DEC Rainbow 100

In 1960, Digital Equipment Corporation (DEC) set the computing world on its ear by introducing a small computer at an outrageously low cost. Computing power had come within the reach of thousands more. The cost? A mere $120,000.

Today Digital is about to do it again, with a line of small computers that will put computing within the reach of thousands — perhaps millions — more.

These four machines are the Rainbow 100 (also known as the PC100), the DECmate II (also known as the PC200), the Professional 325 (PC325), and the Professional 350 (PC350).

The one I find most exciting is the Rainbow.

The Rainbow comes with a black & white screen that displays 24 lines of either 80 or 132 characters. (The

screen switches easily between the two.) The keyboard is detachable and excellent. It ties with the TeleVideo keyboard as my favorite. (The *my* in "my favorite" is very important — you certainly might prefer others.) The keyboard is detachable. It has a numeric keypad (with add, subtract, multiply, and divide symbols), separate cursor movement keys, and more special function keys than one is ever likely to need (there are 36 extra keys on the keyboard).

The shift key, like on the IBM, is not directly next to the "Z." It is, however, larger than any other keys around it, and adjusting to the new placement is not a major hardship.

The disk drives are double disk drives, each holding two 5¼-inch disks. Each disk holds 400K of information, for a total of 800K.

The Rainbow is an 8 *and* a 16-bit machine. It will run either CP/M or CP/M-86 software. For $250 more you can run programs in the MS-DOS (IBM-DOS) format. 64K of RAM is standard. It is expandable to 256K

The cost is $3,495. Quite a value.

The word processing program chosen by Digital for the Rainbow is Select. I guess we can allow them one mistake. Actually, Select is a good choice for executives who type two letters per week, and maybe that's who they thought would be buying the Rainbow. I am also told the Select offered for the Rainbow is "enhanced." Well, for $595, the enhanced Select would have to be awfully enhanced. In the mean time, it's good to know that almost any word processing program will run, and run well, on the Rainbow.

Digital gives away, for free, a book on personal computing (an embarrassment to those of us who *sell* books at $9.95 per. How would Digital like it if I started giving away *computers* for free?) The book is nonetheless recommended reading for anyone considering a computer — Digital or any other.

On the cover is a photo taken from high above an executive-engineer type, a keyboard sort-of on his lap. The man is looking directly at the photographer with a what-the-hell-are-you-doing-up-there? look on his face. Inside the book, for those concerned about Digital's solvency, is a photo of a building — only slightly smaller than the Great Wall of China — labeled "Digital Equipment Corporation, Parker Street facility."

You can write to them at Parker Street and request your copy. (*Digital Equipment Corporation, Media Response Manager, 129 Parker Street, Maynard, Massachusetts, 01754*) Ask for the book "Guide to Personal Computing."

DECmate II

This is very much like the Rainbow, except the processor is the Digital 6120, which is designed to run Digital's existing word processing program. It is (get this) a *twelve*-bit processor (just when I was getting used to eight and sixteen). But don't worry: for $495 you can have a CP/M auxiliary processor installed and run 8-bit CP/M programs just like everybody else. The CP/M plug-in card also adds an additional 64K of RAM.

The DECmate II, with the word processing software,

is $3,745. This would give you a superior stand-alone word processor, for a fraction of the traditional Wang-Lanier-IBM Displaywriter (etc.) stand-alone price.

The word processing program on the DECmate II is powerful and easy to use. It includes dandy features like the display of bold face letters in bold and underlined words underlined on the screen.

For an additional $500 you get a List, Sort, Math, and Communication add-on program that provides sophisticated list management, sorting features, math functions, and a complete communications package.

This is a top-of-the line word processing program, tailor-made for an excellent machine. It directly rivals the $8,000 to $15,000 stand alone word processors sold by The Other Guys. (Only a few months ago it *was* one of the $8,000 to $15,000 stand alone word processors!) It should certainly be considered if you're planning to spend more than $4,000 on your word processing computer.

VICTOR 9000

Victor is a name more commonly associated with adding machines than computers. This is understandable, since the Victor Adding Machine Company has been around almost as long as the Victor Talking Machine Company. Well, the Victor Talking Machine Company became RCA Victor and the Victor Adding Machine Company became Victor Business Products and Victor Business Products has just released an excellent computer.

The Victor 9000 is a state-of-the-art personal computer: 128K RAM, detachable keyboard, 24 eighty-character lines, and two 5¼-inch disk drives, each holding a whopping 620K of information. (Expandable to 1,200K per drive!)

The screen display is the sharpest and, to my taste, most agreeable of any personal computer. Each character is not only sharp and clear, but is also made up of thicks and thins, very much like a typeface used in printing. The video screen tilts up and down, left and right for maximum operator comfort. The computer has full graphics capabilities.

The keyboard has not only a ten-key numeric keypad,

but also a full function calculator. (Well, what would you expect from the Victor Adding Machine Company?) In the midst of any program you can enter the calculator mode, calculate, and then return to the program. This may sound flashy, but a $5.95 handheld calculator glued onto your keyboard would perform essentially the same task.

The Victor 9000 is a 16-bit computer, and all of the

current software limitations regarding the IBM personal computer would apply to the Victor 9000.

A company is making a plug-in card for the Victor 9000 that allows it to run any standard 8-bit CP/M program. This $600 card removes my major concern about the Victor: lack of software.

Both CP/M-86 and MS-DOS are included in the price. The price, by the way, is $4,995. Although this is the highest-priced computer in this book, it is also the most powerful and, considering the features offered, is a good value. A comparably equipped IBM personal computer, for example, would cost around $6,000. The Radio Shack Model 16, at $4,995, doesn't even come close.

PERIPHERALS

I-PROTECT

If you are concerned about radioactive baddies creeping out of your video screen, here is a solution. It's called I-Protect. (The pun I am sure is intentional.)

I-Protect is a quarter-inch thick piece of lead-impregnated plastic. Somehow, they have arranged it so that you can see through lead. The I-Protect screen is, in fact, quite transparent. The lead, however, blocks all of the x-rays and most of the ultra violet rays emanating from the video screen. (This type of plastic is used for windows in nuclear power plants.)

The only problem with I-Protect is that the plastic is about as reflective as the Joy-washed dishes that you can see yourself in. ("And that's a nice reflection on you.") This may be valuable when writing self portraits but, save that, reflected glare is about as troublesome in the short run as radiation might be in the long run.

The I-Protect people are about to solve this problem by laminating a Polaroid filter to the I-Protect shield. In the near future, and for less than $150, you should be able to have the best of both worlds: protection and Polaroid.

I have no idea how real all this radiation danger from video screens is. It will take years of statistical analysis to come to a conclusion. In the meantime, if all it takes is $150 to avoid becoming a statistic, I find that inexpensive insurance. Like my morning handful of vitamins, I may not need any of them during a given day, but I take them anyway, just in case.

Perfect Data Head Cleaner

Cleanliness is vital to the correct functioning of disk drives. Not only must the disks be kept free of fingerprints and coffee spills, the read/write heads must be occasionally cleaned for optimum performance.

A complete head cleaning takes about a minute, and a head cleaning kits costs about $30 — a worthwhile expenditure of both time and money.

A major manufacturer of head cleaning disks is Innovative Computer Products, makers of PerfectData. Everyone from Burroughs to Radio Shack to Xerox buys head cleaning kits from Innovative to market under their own name.

Dvorak Keyboard Software

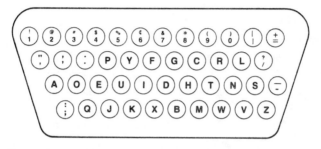

It seems that back in 1873, there was a major problem with typewriters: people typed faster than the machinery could handle. This resulted in a frequent, and annoying, mangling of keys. There was some serious talk of abandoning this newfangled contraption altogether.

Christopher Latham Sholes to the rescue! Chris Sholes did not invent a more efficient typewriter. He invented the *least* efficient placement of keys on the keyboard. He placed the most frequently used letters under the least used fingers. (A and E, for example, under the little and ring fingers of the *left* hand.)

With this intentionally difficult placement of letters on the keyboard, typists seldom overloaded the meager capacity of these early typewriters, and the Machine Age entered the office.

As typewriter mechanisms improved, the keyboard did not change. Mr. Sholes did a good job: his intentionally inefficient keyboard has plagued typists for more than a century.

In the early 1930s, August Dvorak introduced a "simplified" keyboard, one that placed the most often used letters under the most often used fingers.

Following World War II there was a lot of talk

about the Dvorak keyboard, but the typists who knew the old keyboard were, for the most part, unwilling to learn a new one — even one that promised to increase the speed and ease of typing. The Simplified Keyboard fell into disuse.

There has remained a small but loyal following of Dvorak users, much like the Esperantists. One of their main problems was a lack of typewriters. (For the Dvoraks, not the Esperantists.) For a while only Smith Corona made a typewriter with a Dvorak keyboard.

Personal computers, however, might bring the rebirth of the Simplified Keyboard. With the right software, the keys on almost any personal computer can be reprogrammed to conform to the Dvorak standard. Rearranging the plastic keys, by pulling them off and replacing them or by gluing new letters over the old, completes the transformation.

Many people attracted to word processing on personal computers have never typed before. They must learn *some* system of typing: might as well be the Dvorak system as any other. Further, these people are generally not concerned about using their typing as a marketable skill. They are therefore not concerned that learning the Dvorak keyboard will not help them get a secretarial job.

I do not use the Dvorak keyboard. I am a hunt-and-peck typist, and I hear that we are the hardest to retrain. (Touch-typists can relearn the Dvorak keyboard without major trauma, I am told.) The idea of the Dvorak keyboard makes sense, though, and the evidence convincing. Were I learning typing for the first time, I would certainly consider learning Dvorak.

For more information on the Dvorak keyboard, you can send $6 to Philip Davis (*Box 643, West Sacramento, California, 95691*) and ask for a reprint of the article "There is a Better Typewriter Keyboard," and a sample copy or two of his quarterly Dvorak newsletter *Quick Strokes.*

For information on software that will turn your personal computer into a Dvorak personal computer, you can contact Nick Hammond at FBN Software.

D-Cat Modem

When it came time to transmit the text in this book from my computer to the typesetter over telephone lines, a modem was needed. I felt duty-bound to try the least expensive modem advertised, which was $99. If it worked I could recommend it. (Modems are very straight forward. They either work or they don't. Nothing very subjective about them.)

Well, for three painful days I tried to get the $99 modem to work on either of two computers I have. Nothing. The people at the $99 modem company were very nice, but everything they suggested failed to work. (I must have heard the man say, "I can't understand it" more times than I heard Nixon say, "I am not a crook.")

Deadlines were broken left and right. The typesetters were very kind, far more patient than I. Finally I called for help outside the $99 modem company. Brian, my technical ace in the hole, arrived. and plugged in a D-Cat modem. It worked perfectly first time. It has continued to work perfectly throughout the transmission of the entire text.

D-Cat is made by Novation, a company that has been in the modem business for a number of years. They know modems.

The D-Cat is $199. After what I went through with the $99 modem, I can recommend — with not only enthusiasm but gratitude — that you spend twice as much for a D-Cat.

Those who have purchased — or are considering the purchase — of a TeleVideo 802 may want to get a program from New Generation Systems (*2153 Golf Course Drive, Reston, VA, 22091, 703-476-9143*). It allows for easy programming of the programmable function keys, which eases the operation of many programs. It also works with all TeleVideo 950 terminals, and retails for $75.

As I mentioned at the start of this chapter, the world of computer hardware and software is changing at a remarkable rate. It's interesting to consider that with all it has to offer, the personal computer industry is less than seven years old.

If you're planning to purchase a personal computer for word processing any time after May 1, 1983, please write and ask for **The Word Processing Book UPDATE #4.** (Updates #1, #2 and #3 have already been incorporated into this text.) It's free, but please enclose a double-stamped, self-addressed envelope. If you want to include a dollar or two to help pay for printing, that would be appreciated, although certainly not necessary.

Please be sure to mention **The Word Processing Book**, as we issue updates for **The Personal Computer Book** as well.

Peter A McWilliams
Box 69773
Los Angeles, California
90069

Your questions and comments are welcome. Although I cannot promise a personal reply, questions of general interest will be answered and printed in UPDATE #4 and in future editions of this book, so please write.

And now it's time to move ahead to the final chapter and the last frontier, **Purchasing a Word Processing Computer.**

Chapter Fourteen

Purchasing a Word Processing Computer

How does one go about purchasing a word processing computer? The same way porcupines and Catholics make love: very carefully. Pretend you were about to buy your first car and you knew something about cars, but you'd never driven one; you did not, in fact, even know quite what they look like. You would have many automobile showrooms to visit, each full of bright-to-surly salespersons, each claiming that his or her car was *the* car.

The analogy of buying-a-computer-is-like-buying-a-car breaks down at a certain point. The fact is, more often than not, buying a computer is like joining a religion. If you ask people what they think about their computer it's a lot like asking people what they think about God. Expect emotionally charged and not necessarily coherent replies. Some will proselytize; others will find discussing It "too personal." Some are wide-eyed with enthusiasm; others are silent with serene Knowing. Some believe their computer is the One Way, the Right Way, and the Only Way; others accept that there are many paths to RAM.

You'll find this attitude among friends who own computers (the "converts"), the people who sell them (the "preachers"), and those of us who write about them (the "Biblical scholars"). Every so often, much to my amazement and amusement, I find myself responding negatively to positive comments about the direct competitor of the computer I own. In actuality I know that there is not one whit of difference between these two machines, but I note the wave of resentment passes over me as I see an advertisement for that "other" machine.

In selecting a computer and selecting a religion I would give you the same advice: Take your time, investigate all claims carefully, don't make any hasty decisions, and remember that it must work for *you*. Take the histrionics of the zealots with more than a few grains of salt. And save some salt for the journey; the road may well be slippery ahead.

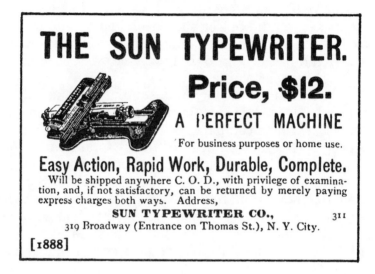
When shopping for a word processing computer, visit not only the popular stores (they'll usually have the word "computer" cleverly used in their name), but investigate, too, computerized office machine stores.

Don't expect too much from computer salespeople. The computer world is growing so quickly that truly knowledgeable people can make several hundred dollars a day as consultants; why on earth should they hang around a computer store at minimum wage in the hope of an occasional commission?

The Peter Principle is rife in computer stores as well: If Tom knows a great deal about computers and how to sell them, he soon becomes the store manager. Tom knows nothing about scheduling personnel or ordering hardware or hiring or supervising, so he spends most of his time doing what he doesn't know how to do. Meanwhile, the bad salespeople never get promoted because they're not very good, but they never get fired for Tom is afraid to make any changes. There certainly are some glowing exceptions to this scenario, but on the whole, visit computer stores to look at computers, not stellar sales techniques.

In all fairness, computerdom is in the midst of an information explosion, one that will be increasing in geometric proportions for some time to come. An ordinary human being, even one dedicated to learning all he or she can, simply cannot keep up. I can't keep up with the rather narrow field of word processing — and I don't have to wait on customers all day. I can imagine the difficulty someone might have if, in addition to word processing, they were asked to know all about four or five different computers and thirty or forty software programs ranging from general ledger to electronic pinball.

Here are ten suggestions you might want to keep in mind while shopping for your word processing computer.

1. Make an appointment. Most computer stores have their games expert, their accounting expert, their programming expert, etc. Telephone and ask to speak to their word processing expert. Make an appointment with that person. If you walk in cold off the street, the first available salesperson will glom onto you, and if he or she is working on a commission, he or she will not be very willing to unglom, even if his or her total knowledge of word processing can be engraved on the underside of a caraway seed. You'll find this salesperson running to the salesperson who knows about word processing with your questions and returning with broadly interpretive answers. Every time you walk into that store you will "belong" to that unknowing salesperson.

2. Do not be intimidated by jargon. Salespeople who use excessive jargon either know everything about computers and nothing about communication, or they know very little about computers and are trying to conceal that fact. When in doubt about what a word or phrase means, ask. Asking may not do you any good, but don't be afraid to give it a try.

3. See if you can spend some time alone with the computer. This usually isn't too hard to arrange. When you think you know enough to attempt a solo flight all you have to say is, "Why don't you take care of some of your other customers and come back to me later?" There are almost always other customers to be taken care of.

4. Ask for print-outs. It's a good idea to have two or three paragraphs that are the same (Gettysburg Address, Pledge of Allegiance, "Casey At The Bat," anything) so that you can have print outs from several printers of the same material. It's easier to compare print quality when the text is the same.

5. When trying a computer, do the work that you'll be using the computer for. If you're going to use it for creative writing, write something creative. If you're going to use it for correspondence, write letters. (My friends never got more letters than when I was shopping for a computer.) If you'll be using it to transcribe dictation, bring some dictation.

6. Make notes. Write down model numbers, prices, salespeople's names, everything. After leaving the store, debrief yourself and note the pros and the cons of the machines you just evaluated. The things that are clear in your mind upon leaving a store will be hopelessly muddled a few weeks and a dozen computers later. Ask, too, for any printed literature the store can part with.

7. Trust your intuition. It's important that you feel good about the computer you purchase — especially the keyboard and the video screen. Include your emotional reactions in your notes and in your decision. Just as cars are more than how many MPG they get, computers are more than how much RAM they have.

8. What happens if it breaks? Be sure to investigate what you'll have to do if the computer does not compute either in or out of warranty. Can you bring it back to the store or will you have to pack it up and ship it to California? How much time will repairs take? Are loaners available for free or at a reasonable cost? Will the store put all its promises in writing? Think about the unthinkable before you buy.

9. Take your time. Don't try to look at everything in a week. You might experience a personal Systems Overload. Take it easy. If you must travel to The Big City to do your investigations, it's better to plan several shorter trips rather than one long one. Gather all the information you can, let it digest, and make your decision from a calm, neutral frame of mind.

10. Enjoy yourself. Keep in mind that it's hard to lose. Whatever personal computer with word processing capabilities you eventually own will be light years ahead of whatever you're using now, even if it's the finest of electric typewriters. You might not buy the very best computer that fills your every need for the very best price, but so what? Whatever you do buy will serve you faithfully and brilliantly for years to come. Knowing there's no way to lose, enjoy playing one of the most intricate computer games around: buying a computer.

"Hello! I would like to purchase a word processing computer."

"Oh, you have come to the right place, sir. We have a wonderful word processing spinning wheel. On sale."

"But I read this book called **The Word Processing Book** and the author never once mentioned spinning wheels."

"Then the author is a fool! Have you ever read **The Spinning Wheel Book?**"

"No."

"Oh, you have missed so much in life. What do you want a word processor for?"

"To write with."

"How can you hope to write about life if you've never read **The Spinning Wheel Book,** which is on sale, too."

"But the author of **The Word Processing Book** said..."

"Fool! The man is a fool! I do not care what a fool has to say."

"I don't know what to think."

"Think about spinning wheels. Word processing spinning wheels."

"But I don't want a spinning wheel!"

"Then how about a puppy dog? A nice word processing puppy dog..."

You have run the gauntlet and have decided on the software and the hardware that will become your personal word processing computer. What's the best way to go about buying it? Go to the store that sells what you want and write them a check, right? Well, not right away. Eventually, yes, but the *size* of the check is what I would like to explore.

Retail computer stores buy their hardware at 15 to 40%, and their software at up to 50%-off the retail price. If they are asking the full retail price for the equipment you desire, there's no reason why you, too, should not share in the generosity of the original equipment manufacturers. How to do this? Let me begin with a story.

When I was one and twenty and living in Detroit, I had, thanks to the sale of some books, enough money, or at least enough credit, to buy a Mercedes Benz. In 1971, buying a Mercedes in Detroit, Michigan, was about as easy as buying Swiss chocolate in Hershey, Pennsylvania. There were two car dealers that sold Mercedes, one near Grosse Pointe, one near Bloomfield Hills, both owned by the same man.

The reception a 21-year-old pseudo-hippie received in a Detroit, Michigan Mercedes dealership in 1971 was, how you say?, not warm. I have a better chance of getting a ride on the next launching of the Space Shuttle than I had of getting a test drive in a 280 SE.

Finally I met a salesman who was kind to me, who talked to me, who gave me color pictures of Mercedes Benzes and who actually quoted me a price: $9,100. That was the full retail price. I was told that Mercedes were never, ever discounted. It somehow wasn't sophisticated to even discuss such things. Discounts were for people who shopped at K Mart, not Mercedes Benz dealerships.

When the bank approved my loan, several of the salesmen who had initially snubbed me attempted suicide by jumping out the showroom window. The showroom was on the ground floor, so one might question the sincerity of their actions, but it would be safe to say that the emotions in the Mercedes dealership that week ran the gamut from regret to consternation. From that time on, 21-year-old pseudo-hippies were treated with far greater respect in Detroit, Michigan, Mercedes dealerships. But that is not the moral of this story. That is not even the end of this story.

I tried several more times to get some kind of discount, but the dealership held firm: $9,100. I heard about a leasing company in Chicago that sold cars at a discount. I called them on the off chance that they might happen to have a Mercedes Benz 280 SE sitting around. They did. Price: $7,800. Condition: That I pick up the car in Chicago and never darken their door again.

I called my salesman, told him the name of the leasing company, the person I talked to and the price quoted. He said he'd call me back. He did, within ten minutes, and had a new price: $8,100. I accepted. It was worth $300, I felt, to have the use of a local service department, the good will of the dealership, and to ensure that the salesman who had be-friended me would get his commission.

(Epilogue: The Mercedes served me well for eight years. When I bought my next car, in 1979, it was a Honda. Price: $8,100.)

(Epilogue 2: I did not get a discount on the Honda. In

fact, I had to travel to Oregon before I could find a dealer that would sell it to me at list.)

The moral of the story is this: If you casually ask for vague discounts on your computer system you are not likely to get any. If, however, you have a firm quote from a verifiable source, your chance of paying less is greatly increased.

Who will quote you these lower prices? Mail order computer emporiums. Their advertisements populate the back pages of almost every computing magazine (especially *BYTE*). Each specializes in various brand names. Call the ones that carry the equipment you have decided upon and find the best prices. Then you can return to the computer store with precise figures of what the identical equipment can be had for elsewhere.

The store should then be in a position to negotiate. If not, then consider ordering it from the mail order house. If the store is willing to negotiate, do not expect them to meet the price quoted by the mail order company. The retail computer store has overhead, salespeople to pay (including yours), warranties to honor, and so on.

In one sense, computer stores are in a disadvantageous position. People walk in, often knowing nothing about computers; the salespeople teach these customers a great deal about computing and specific products; and the person who once was ignorant now knows just enough to order his or her computer at a discount by mail. Not everyone who enters a retail computer store eventually orders a computer by mail. If they did, computer stores would be, by now, no more. And, clearly, that is not the case.

It is, however, fair to keep in mind that if the computer store were not there you might never have been able to meet the new Love of your Life. That's worth something. Also, the more the store offers in the way of support, service, additional software, computer clubs, lessons, and the like, the more valuable it becomes to purchase from that source.

I have no major recommendation one way or another — mail order or local computer store. If there is nothing much the computer store gave you before the sale, and very little to offer you after the sale, buy it by mail. If there is something the computer store offers, decide what that's worth to you and pay it.

Often it's in follow-up support that computer stores more than earn their mark-up.

Just before making your final purchase I have one last recommendation: hire a consultant. Review the many people you've met in your exploration of word processing computers — salespeople, friends, teachers, anyone — and choose the one who would know the most about the equipment and software you've decided upon. Offer them $25, or more, per hour to consult with you. I know it's a lot, but it will be worth it.

Use your first hour going over your planned purchase. Do you have everything you'll need? Are you buying it at the best price and at the best place? Did you forget anything?

Use the next five hours when your equipment arrives.

Have your consultant show you how to set it up, how to turn everything on, how to copy disks, how to load programs, how to run the word processing program, how to print, where to look in the software documentation for further instructions. Then, on your own, practice.

Have your consultant come back the following day, or the following week, and spend a couple of hours answering questions and demonstrating advanced techniques. Another two hours of occasional, random question-answering by telephone and you should be almost ready to hire yourself out as a consultant.

This scenario, which seems reasonable to me, involved 10 hours of consultation. At $25 an hour, that comes to $250. If you've never operated a computer before, a consultant can be the most valuable peripheral you can buy.

Again, if you're reading this after May 1, 1983 and would like my current recommendations on software and hardware, please send a double-stamped self-addressed envelope (along with a dollar or two to help pay for printing, if you like, although it's certainly not necessary). Please ask for UPDATE #4. The address is:

Peter A McWilliams
Box 69773
Los Angeles, California
90069

I feel like the immigrant who, just after stepping off the boat himself, immediately turned and began welcoming his fellow shipmates to America.

Give me your students, your secretaries,
Your huddled writers
   yearning to breathe free,
The wretched refuse of your Selectric III's.
Give these, the homeless, typist-tossed to me.
I lift my disk beside the processor.

Welcome to Word Processing!

About This Book

This book was written, revised, rewritten, edited, corrected (etc., etc.,) on a NorthStar Horizon computer, a TeleVideo 950 terminal, and an NEC 5510 Spinwriter printer.* WordStar was used for writing and editing. The Word Plus checked for and corrected misspellings. Grammar, punctuation and such was checked by Grammatik.

The text was transmitted via a D-Cat modem to DynaType in Glendale, California. There, through the magic of a Comp/Edit phototypesetter, it was transformed into the type you are reading now.

The wood cuts and steel engravings were taken primarily from the Dover Pictorial Archive series.

The book was printed by BookMasters, Ashland, Ohio.

---

*While still a fine system, this computer/terminal combination represents the state-of-the-art about two years ago. There are better values available today. The NEC 5510 Spinwriter has been replaced by the 7710: the best around.

The author with his first word processor
Christmas, 1956

About The Author

There's little point in being coy and writing a biography in the third person. "Peter A McWilliams was born in Detroit, Michigan..." That sort of thing.

I was, indeed, born in Detroit, Michigan in the summer of 1949. My first writing was at the age of four. It was more plagiarism than writing. I faithfully copied the squiggles and wiggles in a book I found, having no idea what any of it meant. I showed it proudly to my parents.

Thinking I had authored the piece—no mean feat, as I had not yet learned to write—mom and dad were favorably impressed. It was, in fact, the most enthusiasm shown me by my parents since the arrival of my younger brother one long year before. Why for even a moment they thought I had written, "Scarlett O'Hara was not beautiful, but men seldom realized it when caught by her charm as the Tarleton twins were." is beyond me.

After learning I did not originate the piece they were duly disappointed, but it was too late. Somewhere in my four-year-old mind I decided to become a writer, and the rest of my life fell into place.

My love of the written word was such that on Christmas, at the age of seven—when most young boys were petitioning Santa for baseball bats and football helmets—I begged for, and received, a typewriter: my first word processor.

I self-published my first book in 1967. I was seventeen. There were two books actually, a gathering of love verse and a collection of poems on society. The love poems sold better. They sold so well, in fact, that a few years and a few thousand books later I had become, "The best selling poet in America under thirty."

And then, in the same dark month, I became thirty *and* I learned that Richard Thomas (John-Boy Walton, for heaven sakes) had sold more poetry than I. For a while I toyed with the idea of billing myself as, "The second-best selling poet in America under thirty-one," but decided eventually upon, "One of the best selling poets in America."

There are currently nine volumes in the poetry series in print, and they have sold more than 2,500,000 copies.

In 1975 I co-wrote and published **The TM Book**. This rode the popular wave of interest in TM to the top of the *New York Times* bestseller list, where it remained #1 for four weeks. Ours was the first book in more than a year to surpass **The Joy of Sex** in sales. I was expecting the headline "TM is Better Than Sex," but it never came.

In 1976 I revised—-with a psychologist and a psychiatrist — an earlier book I had written. The earlier book, published in 1972, was called **Surviving the Loss of a Love**. The expanded edition I published as **How to Survive the Loss of a Love**. It still sells 8,000 copies per month.

After a disastrous attempt to publish a line of greeting cards, I repaired to California for a few years to lick my wounds. It was there that I studied at the feet of the silicon masters and learned all that I know about word processing— almost all of which is in this book. **The Word Processing Book** is my first book — other than poetry — to be published since **How to Survive the Loss of a Love**.

The publication in late 1982 of **The Personal Computer Book** earned me the title (bestowed by *The Houston Post*), of "The Dr. Spock of Personal Computers." My word.

All of the above adventures are painstakingly detailed in my autobiography **In Dubious Talent**. It has yet to be published. It has yet to be written. Finding the time to write these few words was difficult enough. Without my trusty word processor I never would have attempted it.

Thanks for reading **The Word Processing Book**. It was my joy to share it with you.

The author extols the virtues of word processing to an attentive AT&T board meeting

What *Are* Those
Television-Typewriters
Anyway?

The
Personal
Computer
Book

Complete with up to date Brand Name Buying Guide

By the Author of *The Word Processing Book*
Peter A McWilliams

A book about
all the other things
personal computers can do.

The Personal Computer Book is available (hopefully) wherever you purchased your copy of **The Word Processing Book**, or you can order it by mail.

To order by mail, please send $9.95, plus $1.00 for postage and handling, to:

> Ballantine Books
> c/o Random House Mail Service
> 400 Hahn Road
> Westminister, Maryland
> 21157

Or you can order by phone, toll free, and charge the cost of the book (plus shipping) to your Visa, MasterCard, or American Express.

> 800-638-6460
> (In Maryland, please call 800-492-0782)

Please give them the ISBN Number of **The Personal Computer Book** (345 31106-X) and the expiration date of your credit card. (If you would like to order additional copies of **The Word Processing Book**, the ISBN Number is 345 31105-1)

Please include sales tax where applicable and allow 3 to 4 weeks for delivery.

Thank you.

Addresses

Here, in no particular order, are the addresses of the
manufacturers mentioned in this book.

Apple Computer
10260 Bandley Drive
Cupertino, California
95014
(408) 996-1010

Otrona Corporation
(Makers of the Attache Computer)
4755 Walnut Street
Boulder, Colorado 80301
(303) 444-8100

TeleVideo
1170 Morse Avenue
Sunnyville, California
94086

Smith-Corona
65 Locust Avenue
New Canaan, Connecticut
06840
(203) 972-1471

John-Roger
(Author or *A Consciousness
of Wealth*)
Published by
Baraka Books
3500 West Adams
Los Angeles, California
90018

Radio Shack
Fort Worth, Texas
76102

Epson America, Inc.
(Epson dot matrix printer)
3415 Kashiwa Street
Torrance, California
90505
(213) 539-9140

Sony Corporation
(Typecorder)
Office Products Division
9 West 57th Street
New York, New York
10019

Heathkit Electronics Corporation
(Heath H-89)
P.O. Box 167
St. Joseph, Michigan
49805

Zenith Data Systems
(Zenith Z-89—-assembled
version of Heath H-89)
1000 Milwaukee Avenue
Glenview, Illinois
60025

Xerox Corporation
Stamford, Conn.
06904
(203) 329-8700

Atari, Inc.
1265 Borregas Avenue
Sunnyvale, California
94086
(408) 745-2213

Interface Age
(Magazine)
P.O. Box 1234
Cerritos, California
90701

Non-Linear Systems
(KayPro II)
533 Stevens Avenue
Solana Beach, California
92075
(714) 755-1134

DynaType
(Computerized typesetting from
word processors through modems)
740 E. Wilson Avenue
Glendale, California
91206
213-243-1114

BookMasters
(Book printers)
830 Claremont Avenue
Ashland, Ohio
44805
(800) 537-6727

Xedex Corporation
(Makers of Baby Blue for IBM)
1345 Avenue of the Americas
New York, New York
10105

WP News
(A word processing newsletter)
1765 North Highland #306
Hollywood, California
90028

Commodore Computer Systems
681 Moore Road
King of Prussia, Pennsylvania
19406

BYTE
(Magazine)
P.O. Box 590
Martinsville, New Jersey
08836

North Star Computers, Inc.
14440 Catalina Street
San Leandro, California
94577
(415) 357-8500

Oasis Systems
(The WORD and The WORD Plus)
2765 Reynard Way
San Diego, California
92103
(714) 291-9489

Lifeboat Associates
(Software distributor)
1651 Third Avenue
New York, New York
10028

Ring King Visibles, Inc.
(Makers of disk storage files)
215 West Second Street
Muscatine, Iowa
52761
(800) 553-9647

MicroPro International
(WordStar and other software)
1229 Fourth Street
San Rafael, California
94901
(415) 457-8990

Peachtree Software
(PeachText and other software)
3 Corporate Square
Suite 700
Atlanta, Georgia
30329
(404) 325-8533

JMM Enterprises
(They sell adapters
  for the Osborne)
P.O. Box 238
Poway, California
92064
(714) 748-8329

Novation
(Makers of the D-Cat modem)
18664 Oxnard Street
Tarzana, California
91356
(800) 423-5410
(In California: 213-996-5060)

Discount Software
(Software at Discounts)
6520 Selma Avenue
Suite 309
Los Angeles, California
90028
(213) 837-5141

Dover Publications
(Publishers of the
Dover Archive Series)
180 Varick Street
New York, New York
10014

Select Information Systems
(Makers of Select and an
interactive tutorial on
how to use CP/M.)
919 Sir Francis Drake Boulevard
Kentfield, California
94904
(415) 459-4003

NEC Information Systems, Inc.
(Spinwriter letter quality printer)
5 Militia Drive
Lexington, Massachusetts
02173
(617) 862-3120

Muse Software
(Word processing for Apples)
330 North Charles Street
Baltimore, Maryland
21201

Victor Business Products
(Victor 9000)
3900 North Rockwell St.
Chicago, Illinois
60618

The Source
(Data Bank)
1616 Anderson Road
McLean, Virginia
22102

CompuServe
(Data Bank)
Available at any Radio Shack
Computer Center

Personal Computing
(Magazine)
4 Disk Drive (cute, huh?)
Box 1408
Riverton, New Jersey
08077

Creative Computing
(Magazine)
Box 789-M
Morristown, New Jersey
07960

Aspen Software
(Grammatik)
Box 339
Tijeras, New Mexico
87059
(505) 281-1634

Information Unlimited Software
EasyWriter II
281 Arlington Avenue
Berkeley, California
94707

Popular Computing
(Magazine)
P.O. Box 307
Martinsville, New Jersey
08836

IBM
Information Systems Division
Entry Systems Business
(I have no idea what the
last six words mean)
P.O. Box 1328
Boca Ratan, Florida
33432

WordPlay
Document Processing Center
(They rent word processors
  by the hour)
9037 Melrose
Los Angeles, California
90069
(213) 859-1221

Cromemco
280 Bernardo Avenue
Mountain View, California
94043
415-964-7400

Small Systems Engineering
(CP/M Card for Victor 9000)
1056 Elwell Court
Palo Alto, California
94303
415-964-8201

Toshiba America
Information Systems Division
2441 Michelle Drive
Tustin, California
92680
714-730-5000

Eagle Business Systems
28362 Marguerite Parkway
Mission Viejo, California
92692
714-831-8810

Jonos Ltd.
(Escort)
920-C E. Orangethrope
Anaheim, California
92801
714-871-1082

Dynax
(Distributor of
Brother printers)
333 South Hope Street
Suite 2800
Los Angeles, California
90071

Digital Equipment
    Corportation (DEC)
2 Mt. Royal Avenue
Marlboro, MA
01752

Osborne Computer Corporation
26500 Corporate Avenue
Hayward, California
94545
(415) 887-8080

Daisywriter
3540 Wilshire Blvd.
Los Angeles, California
90010
213-386-3111

Franklin Computer
(Makers of ACE 1000)
7030 Colonial Highway
Pennsauken, New Jersey
08109
609-488-1700

Bytewriter
125 Northview Road
Ithaca, New York
14850
607-272-1132

Lexisoft
(Spellbinder)
Box 267
Davis, California
95617
916-758-3630

FYI
(SuperFile)
Box 10998
Austin, Texas
78766
512-346-0133
800-531-5033

Innovative Computer Products
(Perfect Data Head Cleaner)
18360 Oxnard Street
Tarzana, California
91356
213-996-4911

Langley-St. Clair
(I-Protect Radiation Shield)
132 West 24th Street
New York, New York
10011
212-989-6876

Sanyo
51 Joseph Street
Moonachie, NJ
07074

Sony Microcomputer
   Products Division
(Sony Computers)
7 Mercedes Drive
Montvale, NJ
07645

Hewlett Packard
1430 East Orangethorpe Avenue
Fullerton, California
714-870-1000

Lanier Business Products
1700 Chantilly Drive Northeast
Atlanta, Georgia
30324
800-241-1706

FBN Software
(Dvorak Keyboard Software)
1111 Saw Mill Gulch Road
Pebble Beach, California
93953
408-373-5303

Lifetree Software
(VolksWriter for IBM)
177 Webster Street
Suite 342
Monterey, California 93940.

Screenplay Systems
(Scriptor)
211 East Olive Avenue
Suite 203
Burbank, California
91502
213-843-6557

Perfect Software, Inc.
(Perfect Writer)
1400 Shattuck Avenue
Berkeley, California
94709

Morrow Designs
(Morrow Micro Decision)
600 McCormick Street
San Leandro, California
94577
415-430-1970

Digital Marketing
(Micro Link II)
2670 Cherry Lane
Walnut Creek, California
94596

Teleram
2 Corporate Park Drive
White Plains, New York
10604
914-694-9270

Dictronics
(The Random House Thesaurus)
362 Fifth Avenue
New York, New York
10001
(212) 564-0746

For information about **The McWilliams Letter** ("Some's News, Some's Not"), an informal ten-times-per-year update on the world of personal computers, please write to:

Prelude Press
Box 6969B
Los Angeles, California
90069

We'll send you a "descriptive brochure" (as they say in the travel industry).

Thank you.

The Pharaoh's daughter finds a word processor floating in the stream.